Struggles for Power in Early Christianity

STRUGGLES FOR POWER IN EARLY CHRISTIANITY

A Study of the First Letter to Timothy

ELSA TAMEZ

Translated from Spanish by Gloria Kinsler

ORBIS BOOKS
Maryknoll, New York 10545

Library of Congress Cataloging-in-Publication Data

Tamez, Elsa.
    [Luchas de poder en los orígenes del Cristianismo. English]
    Struggles for power in early Christianity : a study of the first letter to Timothy / Elsa Tamez ; translated from Spanish by Gloria Kinsler.
       p. cm.
    Includes bibliographical references and index.
    ISBN-13: 978-1-57075-708-2 (alk. paper)
    ISBN-10: (invalid) 1-57075-710-5 (alk. paper)
    1. Bible. N.T. Timothy, 1st—Criticism, interpretation, etc. I. Title.
BS2745.52.T3613 2007
227'.8306—dc22
                                 2006030804

To Irene Foulkes
Teacher, Colleague, and Friend

Contents

Foreword by Juan José Tamayo   xi

Preface to the English Edition   xv

Introduction   xvii

Chapter 1
**The Rich and the Struggles for Power
in the Christian Community**   1
  Rich Women and the Struggles for Power   2
    The Text: 1 Timothy 2: 8–3:1a   2
    Against Expensive Clothing   4
    An Attack against Wealthy Women   7
    The System of Patronage   9
  The Wealthy Should Not Expect to Be Rewarded
    for Their Favors   11
    The Text: 1 Timothy 6:17-19   11
    *Associations and the Christian Community
      in 1 Timothy*   14
  Godliness Is Not a Means of Gain   16
    The Text: 1 Timothy 6:3-10   16
    Money, Godliness, and Other Teachings   19
    The Wealthy, Godliness, and the Struggles for Power   22

Chapter 2
**The Patriarchal Household and Power Relations
between Genders**   26
  The Cultural Background of the Greco-Roman
    Imperial Patriarchal Society   27
    The Family in the Empire   27

The Domestic Codes   29
The Houses Where Families Lived   30
The Cultural Values of Honor and Shame   32
The Patriarchal Household as an Ideal
      for the Concept of Family   33
Against Women Who Teach and Have Authority
      over Men   35
The Text: 1 Timothy 2:8-12   35
The Salvation of Women through Childbearing   40
The Text: 1 Timothy 2:13–3:1a   40
The Option for Poor but Obedient Widows   47
The Text: 1 Timothy 5:3-16   47
Widows in Antiquity   50
An Order of Widows   51
Rules for Donations for Widows and
      for the Order of Widows   52

Chapter 3
Theological Positions and the Struggles for Power   57
The Diversity of Theological Positions in the Midst
      of Power Struggles   58
The Conditioning of the Imperial Roman Society   65
The Theological Response of the Letter to the
      Internal and External Conflicts   68
God and Jesus Christ Are the Saviors   70
Godliness as a Condition for Salvation   73
The Church and Its Leaders as the Guarantee of the
      Knowledge of the Truth for Salvation   77
An Opening That Excludes and an Option
      for the Poor Conditioned on Obedience   81
Between Intolerance and Useless Divergences   84

Chapter 4
Criteria for Leadership in the Struggles for Power   89
Leadership Positions in the Beginnings of the
      Christian Communities   89
The Supervisor, the College of Presbyters, and
      the Struggles for Power   93

Requirements to Be a Supervisor: Who Is Excluded? 97
  The Text: 1 Timothy 3:1-7 97
Requirements to Be Deacons:
  Who Is Excluded? 105
  The Text: 1 Timothy 3:8-12 105

Conclusion **111**

Appendixes
  I. The Socioeconomic Structure
      of the Roman Empire 115
  II. Acts of Paul and Thecla 116
  III. Plurality in Primitive Christianity 129
  IV. The First Letter to Timothy (complete text) 130

Notes **137**

Bibliography **151**

Index of Biblical Passages **155**

Index of Names and Subjects **158**

Foreword

Neither normative nor absolute rejection,
but reconstruction and dissent

It is my pleasure to present this book of Elsa Tamez, a longtime Latin American theologian and close friend, with whom I have shared—always in tune—not a few debates in different theological settings in Latin America and Europe. Her present work is a thought-provoking study of the First Letter to Timothy, which is usually dated at the end of the first century or the beginning of the second century and is important for understanding the process of the formation of the institutionalization, hierarchicalization, and patriarachalization of the Christian communities. It takes its place among the diverse investigations on the origins of Christianity carried out by different disciplines, all complementary: social historical, political, economic, sociological, cultural anthropological, and so on.

Tamez's analysis centers on the *struggles for power in primitive Christianity provoked by the social stratification of members of the community, by the conflictive relations between the genders and between masters and slaves, and by competition for community leadership and power among different theologies and lifestyles within the community.* One of the principal merits of the book precisely lies in the collation of the category of gender with social position and with leadership status of the simple believer in the Christian community. Generally, studies of this type are centered on only one area and operate with one hermeneutical category, with debatable and undoubtedly reduced results.

Its merit is also to tackle the struggles for power in nascent Christianity, which are usually avoided in many New Testament studies, where a more idyllic and angelic vision of the beginnings of the Christian religion is offered, more with an apologetic sense than with scientific rigor, more with theological prejudices than with historical analysis, and more with a superficial reading than with a hermeneutical critique.

This work first studies the struggles for power motivated by the social position within the system of patronage, consistent with an interchange of relationships between unequals, which was the essence of the asymmetric relationship of patron and client. It dealt with a fundamental pillar of Roman society that was very present in the Christian communities. In the application of that system, rich men and women exercised a powerful influence, even more, an undisputed leadership in the communities with a tendency to consider religion a source for obtaining gains. This was contrary to the movement of Jesus understood as a community of equals. Tamez underlines as a central part of her study the critique of the letter's author of the system of patronage in the Christian community and the utilization of religion as a business. For 1 Timothy the love of money is the root of all kinds of evil (6:10). It is precisely the rich persons who teach doctrines incompatible with those of the letter. Consequently, there existed a certain continuity between teaching, love of money, piety, and leadership, which constitutes a perversion of the Christian faith.

Another power struggle analyzed is that between the genders, between men and women. Here the author of the letter assumes and canonizes the Roman household relationships of patriarchal dominance. Imbued with this ideology, he imposes a rigid control over the women of the community, from manner of dress to the prohibition against teaching—for rich women as well as for all the rest. And, more importantly, he grounds the patriarchal ideology theologically through three arguments: the creation of Adam before Eve, her transgression, and the maternal function as a condition of salvation. To understand the focus of the author, Tamez studies the domestic codes of the Roman patriarchal household, which regulated the relationships and behavior of the household members and the cultural values of honor and shame.

The third type of struggle studied is that which takes place between different theological positions that are present within the community. Tamez discusses in detail the different theologies and the attitude of each toward the poor; she examines the theology of the author and his attitude of tolerance or intolerance of other distinct proposals, using the excellent study of the Costa Rican philosopher Ángel Ocampo, *Los límites de la tolerancia y el sujeto universal, De paradojas y bandidos* (The Limits of Tolerance and the Universal Subject, of Paradoxes and Bandits). The attitude of 1 Timothy cannot be called precisely intolerant, but "patriarchal authoritarianism." His theology is not very innovative; what he does is to assimilate the cultural values of Roman society and to give them a normative value in the Christian community.

There is also a fourth type of struggle for power, which has to do with leadership positions: overseer or *episkopos*, deacons, and elders. 1 Timothy establishes some criteria for the exercise of leadership in these struggles for power. But there is no significant element that would lead to a democratic organization, unlike other texts in the New Testament that are favorable to the participation of believers in decision making and in the co-responsibility of the community, all of it part of ministry. Only the authoritarian and patriarchal exercise of the ecclesiastical leadership is valued.

What has interested me most about this book is the methodology that combines the *reconstruction* of the context in order to understand the why of certain texts and certain ecclesial practices with distance and *dissent*. It is necessary to reconstruct when the author's particular ideology, reflecting patriarchal and discriminatory cultural traditions, clashes with the gospel of Jesus of Nazareth. Dissent does not mean lack of respect for the text. Elsa Tamez combines dissent with an attitude of openness toward those texts that move within the best liberating and egalitarian traditions of the New Testament. It is not possible to read and interpret 1 Timothy outside of the circumstances in which it was written, nor is it possible to impose it mimetically as valid in every time, place, and culture. Therefore, it is neither normative nor absolute rejection but a contextualized reading. With this methodology, important advances gained in the study of the New Testament should be read with the creative use of the hermeneutical circle.

Juan José Tamayo
University Carlos III (Madrid)

Preface to the English Edition

Today, both secular and religious discourse are conditioned by the fear of terrorism. This discourse shows itself to be inadequate, contrived, non-stop, and absolute. It is authoritarian and crushing, leaving no space to consider mature and reasonable alternatives. It provides a sense of security to a people who feel vulnerable and want to be told what to do. But this comes at the price of restrictions on personal and communal freedom, and the generation of hostility between different social groups.

In antiquity, too, there were rhetorical and authoritarian discourses. Many of these were conditioned by distinct factors, such as the fear of undermining certain positions considered to be true, or the fear that new sectors would displace those who occupied positions of authority, or the fear that internal tensions could endanger a community's survival. The First Letter to Timothy is one of those discourses that is explained by its own very particular situation. Internal tensions, struggles for power, threats to the community's survival in an adverse context—these are some of the factors that motivated the author to create a closed and authoritarian discourse that was especially detrimental to women and slaves and to those who thought differently.

When we analyze the letter, seeking to understand the situation behind the text, it becomes a very interesting document, precisely because it portrays situations common to the early church. It reveals the social struggles—particularly struggles for power—present in the beginning of the church and how they received theological legitimation. At the same time, it deals with a situation not very different from the reality of churches today. Today's intraecclesial and interecclesial struggles for power, exclusion, and marginalization reflect the same human condition that was present in 1 Timothy. Nevertheless, the Spirit always acts within human history. From the mirror of 1 Timothy we can see ourselves more clearly, and the situation of our churches today. That should help us to find those criteria that bring us closer to the human face of Jesus Christ and to overcome our own desires for power and domination.

I would like to give many thanks to my friend Gloria Kinsler for the English translation. She knows my way of thinking and writing very well, as we have worked together for many years.

Elsa Tamez

Introduction

The First Letter to Timothy, as well as the letter to Titus and the First Letter of Peter, are New Testament writings that are not used in Latin American circles of community reading[1] of the Bible. And when these letters are used, only the interesting texts are read, such as 1 Timothy 4:12: "Let no one despise your youth, but set the believers an example in speech, in love, in faith, in purity," without taking into account the conflictive and apologetic context in which these words are found. We avoid, or just pass over, certain texts in the same letter that prejudice the excluded, such as women and slaves.

The reason these writings are avoided is obvious. The reading of the Bible from the perspective of the excluded does not find in this letter, or in some other biblical books, words of courage and hope that would animate people to overcome and resist the difficult life that confronts them in the midst of poverty and discrimination. Various verses in 1 Timothy can be singled out as contributing to this idea; the most problematic are those which speak about women, for example, 1 Timothy 2:11-12:

> Let a woman learn in silence with full submission. I permit no woman to teach or to have authority over a man; she is to keep silent.

In our Christian communities and in neighborhood committees, for example, women are a very important axis. Women are the ones who direct, sustain, and animate the community most of the time. To read the letter of 1 Timothy and to obey it without discernment would be to take a step backward, to be silent and follow ideals that in everyday practice do not fit. We could say the same about the condition of exploitation and marginalization of men and women who are lucky enough to be employed or underemployed. Necessity obliges them to obey the boss quietly, even in minimal and sometimes indecent demands, as we have heard in so many testimonies. To read this letter without any critique—that slaves consider their masters worthy of all honor and if the master is a believer they should serve them even more (see 6:1-2)—can be seen not only as biblical legitimation of inhuman situations but as a great absence of God, who is known to be in solidarity with the poor and in whom they have placed their hopes for liberation.

In addition, certain texts are worrisome in that they pass judgment with intolerance on different customs and theological thoughts (1:3-4; 4:1-3), and other texts present a fierce defense of tradition (1:10b, 20; 6:20), as if the new were always bad. The call to defend a doctrine using military images of fighting against an enemy (1:18; 6:12) is frightening. The horrors of the Crusades, the Inquisition, the burning of heretics, excommunications, murderous betrayals, and demonization for thinking differently come to mind when these texts of intolerance are read with a threatening tone.

The instructions on the qualities of leadership that appear in 1 Timothy 3:1-7 would also be uncomfortable for the Christian communities that use a democratic model. In the first place, the tradition of the institutional church has wanted to read in those instructions the installation of a hierarchal power, in which the overseer (*episkopos*) is the bishop, and to him all other leaders and members of the Christian community must submit. Second, the qualities that are assigned principally to the overseer (*episkopos*) coincide with the values of the patriarchal household in which the *paterfamilias* established the authority (vertical) and the difference between persons (superiority) and this was imposed over the wife, children, and slaves. Moreover, these instructions pertained more to the rich because they had houses and slaves.

These are some of the reasons that these texts have not been studied in communitarian Bible reading. People want a God who is on their side, because society seems to be against them. Unlike the Gospels, the prophetic books, Exodus, Revelation, and Psalms—biblical books in which the strong voice of a solidary God is most heard—it seems as if 1 Timothy hides that voice. As scholars who work with the Bible from a liberating perspective, few of us have been keen to interpret 1 Timothy.[2] Actually, many times we hide it, silence it, and when simple women of the community ask us about it, we totally relativize it. We say it is not normative, and we turn their thoughts to other more important and contrary texts such as Galatians 2:28 or the movement of Jesus and his treatment of women. But in reality, many persons with an ingenuous and sincere heart are accustomed to seeing in the Bible a writing to be interpreted literally, written with the inspiration of the Holy Spirit. They believe the Bible is normative and suffer because they do not understand why "God changed his position" in these texts. Other people just get angry—angry because they know that the letter has always been normative during the centuries of church history. We know that in times of crisis and decisions for ecclesial power, 1 Timothy has the last word. This really means that we have not responded well; we have not been responsible, maybe because our hermeneutics have concentrated on liberating texts, or because within the richness of the Bible we always find different and new senses, or maybe because the appropriate time has not arrived, since everything has its time and its hour, as it says in Ecclesiastes 3:1.

But the time has come. The First Letter to Timothy demands to be read and reread in today's time. But with this text it is not possible to apply the same hermeneutical criteria that we are accustomed to using. In the hermeneutical process "to see, to judge, to act,"[3] the activity "to judge" (analysis of the text) is used to illuminate practice that comes from life and its context. This is the moment in which the Bible is reread with liberating criteria that point out the contrary, adverse reality of the excluded.

This does not happen with 1 Timothy, because in some parts—for example, where it speaks about women and slaves—the adverse reality goes hand in hand with the text. New steps must be added in the hermeneutical process of the analysis of the text. One of those is to understand the text through a reconstruction and to dissent from certain affirmations of the text that contradict the gospel itself. To be able to understand historically and culturally why something is affirmed and to have the freedom to not accept its declarations because, paradoxically, it goes against the will of God in solidarity with the excluded, should be a new step in the communitarian biblical hermeneutics. "To have the capacity to dissent from these parts of the Bible is a profoundly liberating process," said a woman participant in one of the Central American biblical workshops. This is the objective of our book: to reconstruct the situation behind the text to better understand the discourse and to be able to dissent from those parts of the letter that oppress persons and veer away from the principles of the gospel of Jesus Christ.

However, our distancing of this letter and rejecting of those texts mentioned mean that various important and interesting aspects of the letter are not considered. For example, its critique of the wealthy (6:17-19) and wealthy women (2:9), especially those who want to become rich or to keep their wealth (6:9), and the affirmation that "love of money is the root of all kinds of evil" are texts that merit being taken into account. But this cannot be done without considering also the texts that legitimate marginalization and oppression. We will have to do a reading as a whole and consider all the elements in order to comprehend the totality of the letter.

Elisabeth Schüssler Fiorenza, a well-known exegete from the United States, has made a very important affirmation with respect to this letter. According to her, there must be a difference in the meaning of description and prescription.[4] She is correct. This letter is exhortative and persuasive; that is, it gives instructions in a rhetorical discourse[5] about the behavior of the leaders and members in the Christian community of Ephesus. The author does not describe how the community really is, but how they should be according to his vision of the world. It is very probable that women were strong leaders of the community and that slaves behaved as free persons,[6] according to the democratic principles of the Jesus movement that they had heard upon being baptized.[7] It could also be that there were other very attractive theologies for some members of the community, and for that reason the author felt obliged to discredit and demonize them, since he considered them damaging or dangerous.

This is why, for Schüssler Fiorenza, it is very important to do a reconstruction of the situation, because it helps us to be more cautious and suspicious in our response to the declarations of the author's discourse today. In this book we attempt to recreate the situation. Even though we are conscious that whatever inclination we have with respect to the reconstruction is hypothetical, we are sure that the study of the letter that includes this perspective will be much richer and appropriate for the popular, pastoral, or community reading of the Bible. This is the reason that the readers of this book will find a lot of data about the historical context of the first and second centuries.

Although it seems difficult to study these kinds of texts from a liberating perspective—above all because we are not accustomed to doing so—after having introduced ourselves to the world of the letter, we believe it to be possible. It is not a matter of accepting what is said, but of understanding and then dissenting from what is read if it does not reflect the principles of the gospel of the kingdom. In the communal reading of the Bible familiar to those interpreting the texts from their own present contexts, it will not be difficult to observe that many of our communities and local churches have similar conflicts: of class, gender, and different theological and political postures. Neither will it be difficult to find on many occasions the traditional "verticalist" answers from the hierarchy toward these conflicts. This reality helps a great deal in understanding the why of this text, which is very important in the hermeneutical process to convert us into enthusiastic creative and effective readers. By doing this we reduce the fruitless deception—or anger—that has been expressed against this Biblical letter. What we need is creativity rather than deception—and not only in a social reconstruction to understand the text, but in a possible answer, new to the situation in our churches today, in which the liberating principles of the gospel of Jesus Christ will really be affirmed.

Guided by what has been said, we have organized the book into four chapters, in which the historic context of the Greco-Roman empire and the Christian community of 1 Timothy will be simultaneously analyzed. In the first chapter we dedicate ourselves to one of the strongest conflicts that passed through this community: power struggles in relation to social position. In the second chapter we analyze power relations between genders, taking into account the cultural values of the patriarchal Greco-Roman empire. In the third chapter we turn to the internal problem of other teachings that confronted the community, the author's intolerance, and at the same time, the danger of a use-less divergence in a hostile situation. In the fourth chapter we study the new criteria that the author proposes for election to positions of leadership. There we see the relationship of the required qualities to the struggles for power and the negative consequences for women, the poor, and slaves.

Because of the lack of resources in Spanish, most of our sources come from non-Spanish-speaking Europe and North America. However, readers will note that the discussion that has domi-nated the Pastoral Letters[8] in the first world will not be present here guiding and conditioning our work. We are referring to the discussion as to whether 1 Timothy is a letter from Paul or from a later school. Much has been said about that, and even though there exists a certain consensus in placing the letter at the end of the first century or the beginning of the second, signed with Paul's pseudonym[9] (which we accept), the debate is not closed.[10] These discussions are interesting, but it seems to us that, when a writing dedicates itself to defending or attacking Pauline authenticity, a great part of the content is lost sight of. For the communitarian reading of the Bible the literal paternity is not fundamental. The very fact that the letter forms part of the Bible as sacred canon is sufficient for it to be taken seriously, embraced, and discussed.

Neither should we give too much importance to another issue common to the various commentaries on the Pastoral Letters. We are referring to the question whether the letter implies a "bourgeois shift"[11] or the accommodation of the Christian com-munity to the Greco-Roman society.[12] What we are most fun-damentally interested in is not to stay in the past of the text but to advance toward the present in its reading. Our preoccupation is more in tune with how to read these texts in the Christian communities living in the poor countries today, who hope to find in the Bible good news; and a first step that this book wants to offer is to help readers understand the situation of that time through a reconstruction.

In line with the opinion of the majority of the commentators about the authorship of 1 Timothy,[13] we have opted to consider the text to be a production of the end of the first century or beginning of the second century.[14] Further, we do not think it appropriate to study the three Pastoral Letters (1 and 2 Timothy and Titus) as though they were responses to the same situation by the same author. If it seems certain that 1 Timothy and Titus are similar and could have been written by the same hand, 2 Timothy seems to us to be a very different document. Its content, its theology, and its tone suggest that it was a writing born of a prisoner condemned unjustly to death. It represents another literary genre, one that has not even been established as such in the academic debates but that we could call "Prison Letters." If we read the letters written by the German pastor Dietrich Bonhoeffer from prison, of the Brazilian Frei Betto, the South African Nelson Mandela, and the African American Martin Luther King, and many more, as well as certain of Paul's writings from prison (see his Letter to the Philippians), we note various constants that indicate the existence of a literary genre that could be called "Letters from Prison," and we propose that they be analyzed separately.[15] We will only study 1 Timothy in this book.

At the same time, even though we agree with the consensus that 1 Timothy was a writing redacted by an author who used the pseudonym Paul—and therefore the name Timothy would also be a pseudonym because of the late placement of the letter—we believe that the concrete reality that is presented in this letter is not invented but real. We believe that the community, or this kind of community, existed and presented the problems and conflicts that we find in the letter. For this reason, we opt to accept what the text says with regard to Ephesus (see 1:3) as the place where the letter has been sent to the community with instructions of the author, directed to a delegate called Timothy.

One of the most interesting things about 1 Timothy is the diversity in the community's members. Among them, rich women (2:9-10), the wealthy (6:17-19), widows (rich, poor, young, elderly; 5:3-16), those who want to be rich (6:9-10), patrons, believers or not, who own slaves (6:1-2), slaves (6:1-2), and in a very important area, those who have a different theological position with respect to the tradition (1:3-4; 4:17; 6:3-5, 20-21).

An important figure is Timothy, described as a youth (4:12) ordained by the elders (4:14; 1:18) with stomach problems

(5:23), who has the task of easing tensions through the instructions sent to him. The letter deals with a diversity of tensions,[16] not just concerning different doctrinal positions but regarding power struggles of various kinds. We find complicated relations of power between the genders, intertwined with those of the social classes that are presented in the church or Christian assembly. Those who had in some way inherited egalitarian and democratic principles from the Jesus movement have come into conflict with the customs of a society that is profoundly patriarchal and stratified. To deal with this situation will be crucial to the interpretation in this letter.

The structure of 1 Timothy is not easily established with precision. The style of rhetoric and exhortation as well as certain digressions (e.g., 1:8-11, 12-17) and repetitions make it difficult to establish a clear structure. One simple outline could be that which we offer here below, in which instructions to the members for a determined behavior (•) alternate with the criticism of other teachings (>).

Greeting 1:1-2
> A charge to Timothy to confront other teachings 1:3-7.
• Two digressions: about the law (1:8-11) and about Paul (1:12-17—behavior)
> A charge to Timothy to confront other teachings 1:18-20
• Behavior required of the community and of the leadership 2:1–3:13
    For the community 2:1-2a
        Political reason 2:2b
        Theological reason 2:3-7
    For men 2:8
    For women 2:9-12
        Theological reasons 2:13-15
    For the overseer 3:1-7
    For deacons 3:8-10; 3:12-13
    For deaconesses 3:11

Explicit proposal of the letter 3:14-15
> Against other teachings and theological reasons 3:16–4:5
• Behavior required: 4:6–6:2 (continuation)

> For Timothy 4:6–5:2
> For widows 5:3-16
> For overseers 5:17-25
> For slaves 6:1-2

> > Against other teachings 6:3-5
> • Behavior required: 6:6-19 (continuation)
> > For those who want to be rich or to keep their wealth 6:1-10
> > For Timothy 6:11-14
> > > Theological affirmation 6:15-16
> > For the wealthy 6:17-19

> > Against other teachings, final exhortation 6:20-21a

Farewell 6:21b

Even though we propose this structure, our work will not follow this outline or any other. We will not analyze the text as has been commonly done in other biblical commentaries. We will use the whole letter to analyze the struggles for power in the nascent Christian community. More important for us—we reiterate—is the interpretation of the letter, taking into account the reconstruction of its social context. This book is a first step to understanding the letter in its context; a second book is needed that would contribute more to updating the history of the influence and impact of the interpretations that 1 Timothy has prompted until now. It is in our plans to continue this task.[17]

I want to thank the Hans-Sigrist Foundation of the University of Bern for the prize awarded to me, which gave me sufficient time for this investigation. I also am grateful to Irene Foulkes for her contributions and to the popular workshops and courses in which I shared this investigation and learned from the reactions of the participants.

1

The Rich and the Struggles for Power in the Christian Community

It is remarkable that at the beginning (2:9ff.) and end of the letter (6:17-19) there are some not very cordial instructions for the wealthy who belong to the Christian community in Ephesus—at the beginning, rich women; at the end, the rich in general, women and men. In addition, in 6:6-10 our attention is powerfully drawn to an even stronger critique of those persons who want to become rich or to the rich who cling to their wealth.[1] The strong and uncomfortable affirmation that "the love of money is the root of all evil" is mentioned here by the author of the letter. If we observe the epistle as a whole, and certain texts carefully, such as 3:1 and 5:17-25, the radical critique cannot be gratuitous. Behind it there is something that provokes this rhetorical speech. It seems to me that there is a problem of power struggles in the community, in which the wealthy, especially rich women, are an essential part. The suspicion that leads us to think in this manner is illuminated not only from the text itself. In our communities or local churches today, we frequently find that well-to-do members will challenge the leaders of the community, by-passing them to impose their own will. Could it be that something similar is what was happening in the community or communities of Ephesus?

In this section we will analyze some texts that will lead us to confirm our suspicions that there were struggles for power in the Christian community to whom this letter was directed, such as the participation of well-to-do persons in these struggles, and above all between rich women and male leaders of the community. At the same time we will situate these texts in their social and economic context in order to reach some conclusions.[2]

Let us begin with the rich women, because it is one of the most crucial points in the situation of the community.

RICH WOMEN AND THE STRUGGLES FOR POWER

The Text: 1 Timothy 2:8–3:1a

> [8] I desire, then, that in every place the men should pray, lifting up holy hands without anger or argument; [9] also that the women should dress themselves modestly and decently in suitable clothing, not with hair braided, or with gold, pearls, or expensive clothes, [10] but with good works as is proper for women who profess reverence for God. [11] Let women learn in silence with full submission. [12] I permit no woman to teach or to have authority over a man; she is to keep silent. [13] For Adam was formed first, then Eve; [14] and Adam was not deceived, but the woman was deceived and became a transgressor. [15] Yet she will be saved through childbearing, provided they continue in faith and love and holiness, with modesty. [3:1] This saying is sure.

The literary context comes in the middle of the author's instructions begun in chapter 2 with respect to prayer. The instructions are directed first to the whole community:

> [2:1] First of all, then, I urge that supplications, prayers, intercessions, and thanksgiving be made for everyone. . . .

After that come the men (2:8) and finally the women (2:9-15). If we compare the instruction directed to the men with that to the women, we immediately observe a considerable difference between them. The instruction to the men is very brief: to pray serenely with their hands raised, without anger or resentment. That to the women is much longer and very negative: it includes the manner of dressing and how to behave in the Christian community and, implicitly, in the household (2:9-12); besides that, the author adds an interpretation of Scripture (Genesis) that favors the preeminence of the man (2:13-14) and a theological affirmation to legitimate the command (2:15).

The most authoritarian verse is 2:12, in which the author explicitly rejects the idea of a woman teaching (*didaskein*) and "having authority (*authentein*) over a man." He uses the phrase "I do not permit that" (*ouk epitrepō*). When the author gives instructions to the whole community and to the men on their way of praying and to the women on how to dress, he uses two less negative verbs than "I do not permit that." In 2:1 he writes "I exhort . . ." (*parakalō*) when speaking about prayer for all the community, and in 2:8: "I desire" (*boulomai*) in reference to how men should pray and what should be the clothing of the women[3] in the Christian community.[4] These two terms leave room for the possibility of dialogue. "To exhort" (*parakalō*), for example, is a term that supposes "a command in the context of mutual relationships"[5]; it could even be translated "I recommend." The verb "to desire" (*boulomai*), although it could be an imperative, is ambiguous and could leave room for dialogue. "I do not permit" (*ouk epitrepō*), however, is surprisingly authoritarian and closes off dialogue. We could say the same thing of the imperative "to learn" in the phrase "Let women learn in silence with full submission" (2:11). In synthesis, the author prohibits women from teaching or having authority or dominion over men. This prohibition, although surely directed to all the women, is related to or rather is motivated or provoked by certain wealthy women who are asked not to be ostentatious in their dress.

In this situation, the question that comes up is: Why does the author react in this way against this feminine sector of the community? Is it only because he dislikes women, or are there other situations that provoke such a negative and angry demand?

The text is very complex, and the distinct aspects that appear must be defined in order better to understand them. Three elements come to our attention: the first is the social condition of the women who are mentioned here. They are rich, as can be deduced from their clothing (2:9-10). The second element is the condition of the feminine gender itself (2:11-12), in which certain behaviors are demanded according to patriarchal domestic codes of the time, such as keeping silent during instruction, not placing oneself over a man, and subordinating oneself to him (keep silent) (2:12b). The third is the element of maternity with salvific character (2:15), which sends us to the conflict with "other teachings" in 4:3, where we read, "They forbid marriage . . . ." Connected to this dispute about marriage also is the case of young widows in 5:14.

> So I would have younger widows marry, bear children and manage their households, so as to give the adversary no occasion to revile us.

As can be seen, the problem is not simple, because certain diverse issues are woven together that cannot be ignored or reduced to just one issue.

For didactic reasons, in this chapter we will concentrate only on the question of class or social condition of the women mentioned in 2:9-10. We will deal with gender relations (2:13-15) and theological disputes in the following chapters.

Against Expensive Clothing

Reading the letter from our Latin American context, the exhortation on women's clothing gets our attention right away. Above all, the way in which women should *not* dress or adorn themselves. If the text had stopped at the first part, that is, in 2:9a, the social condition of these women would have gone unnoticed. It would have been seen as a normal exhortation within the pietistic tradition that in the house of God the faithful would dress appropriately and modestly (*aidous*) and with good judgment, simplicity, and decency (*sōphrosynēs*). The author does not stop there, however, but adds a lengthy comment about the opposite of this kind of dress. That is, he does not think it is all right to see in the Christian community women with ostentatious hairstyles (or elaborate braids) adorned with gold and pearls or dressed in expensive clothing. The author uses for "ostentatious hair" the Greek word *plegmata*, which literally means "braids." In antiquity, a luxurious or ostentatious hairstyle would consist of very elaborate braids, probably sustained with finely woven nets including broaches of gold and precious stones. Such very sophisticated hairstyles of wealthy women are represented on some ancient reliefs. Pearls, which were much appreciated in the Hellenistic world and in the provinces of Asia, could also refer to earrings, rings, or necklaces.[6] The author contrasts, then, modesty and simplicity (v. 9a) with ostentation (v. 9b).[7] Some commentators believe that this form of luxurious and pompous attire points more to women courtesans or prostitutes rather than wealthy aristocratic women,[8] therefore underlining the question of indecency. But an analysis of the whole letter and its critical vision of the wealthy members of the community supports our reading.

The exhortation to dress in a modest and simple manner, where good works are more important than luxurious attire, cannot be seen simply as a straightforward motif frequent within the moral values of antiquity. Many commentators mention in passing that the advice to dress without ostentation was a common philosophical topic among thinkers and satirists at that time, such as a reference to "the rules of courtesy for decent women." In fact, the satirists Martial and Juvenal made fun of complicated hairstyles and of the extravagant clothing of society's aristocratic women. Advice on modest dress for these rich women is found also in ancient writers such as Plutarch, Pliny, Seneca, and Philo, among others.

Nevertheless, we believe that the author does not come up with this topic out of the air, in passing, to counsel all the women of the Christian community on how they should dress. The reference to sophisticated hairstyles, gold, pearls, and expensive clothing, in a community in which the majority of the members are poor, alerts all readers to pay attention to this point because it gives a crucial clue for the reconstruction of the situation. It raises the possibility that the principal problem that the author brings up is not simply about women in general, leaders of the community, but about rich women (as affirmed by various biblical scholars[9]), women who were probably very dominant, as we will see below. At this time, the end of the first century and the beginning of the second century, the tensions caused by the presence of wealthy men and women intensified within the Christian communities.[10] This growing tension between the different social classes in the community was aggravated when some members appeared in luxurious clothing alongside those who dressed poorly. For this reason, we insist that the principal critique is ostentation, not indecency.

But the fundamental problem is not the manner of dress but the behavior of those wearing the ostentatious clothing. The most profound tensions probably were produced between church leaders and the wealthy believers of the community rather than between the wealthy and those of scarce resources. The clothing simply serves to point out the social differences and, in passing, to observe the rejection of all ostentation.

We now need to clarify two aspects regarding women and social strata or class in antiquity. In the first place, something that is obvious but often overlooked, when a reading is concentrated primarily on gender, independent from class, is that the oppression of women in the Greco-Roman society in many cases was not equal. Poor women suffered a greater oppression because of their gender and their social condition. Rich women enjoyed many more privileges than poor women and men. Thus, women in the various social strata, from the emperor's house to indigent women of the lowest class, experienced different situations. Although it was not always the case, rich and powerful women could be just as oppressive as men of the same stratum.[11]

The second aspect to consider is that to speak of rich members of the community does not imply that we are speaking of the truly wealthy of the Roman empire. As can be seen in Appendix I, there was a great distance between the really rich of the aristocracy, who were the large landowners who possessed wealth, power, and status, and the majority of the population, urban as well as farmers, who were poor. Some were above the poverty line, such as administrators for the wealthy, or religious professionals, but because of the distance of their position from the aristocracy, as well as their small number, they cannot be seen as a middle class. As is emphasized today by different analysts of Roman imperial society, in that time there was no middle class as we now conceive it, where a large part of the population is very visible to those who are wealthier and those who are poorer.[12] In any case what is important here is that the rich women, members of the Christian community in Ephesus, are not the truly rich of the Roman empire. It may be that the rich members did not even form part of the very small number of the Christian sub-decurions ("the little rich" of the provinces who belonged to the city councils and contributed in some way to managing the expenses), but they were in a comfortable position, business administrators of the rich or a trader who had accumulated a certain fortune. Obviously, within the Christian community, their wealth and power became evident as they participated in communities made up mostly of poor persons (not the indigent).[13] Now that we have made these clarifications, we will go on to analyze the text in terms of the power struggles influenced by these social positions.

An Attack against Wealthy Women

Again, the first question that comes to mind is: Why does the author attack the rich women in the community like this? Because they are women? Because they are rich? Both things could be present, because we know that the critical attitude of this letter is not only against the leadership of women but also against the love of money. The phrase "the root of all evil is the love of money" can be a very hard judgment for those who possess wealth. Nevertheless, in 1 Timothy it is not possible to affirm with clarity the author's attitude toward wealthy persons. There is ambiguity in the text: although he combats the love of money, in 6:1-2 he exhorts the slaves to give honor to their masters, who are rich. Nor does he exclude the rich from the community, as occurs in the Letter of James (5:1-6), but he exhorts them to give generously (6:17-19).

L. W. Countryman affirms that in that time the communities had an ambiguous vision of wealth: on one side, they had a strong criticism of wealthy men and women, following the Jewish prophetic heritage; but, on the other side, the need of their donations was becoming more and more necessary in order to help the poor, until they could not do without them.[14] In the writings of Tertullian, Clement, and Origen, for example, we find ambiguity toward the rich and wealth. This indetermination is present also in 1 Timothy. We think that the problem that provokes the letter is caused neither by women in general (although, yes, the author's reaction to women is very negative) nor by the presence of rich women (and men), but the problem is the power and influence that both these elements together have over the community.

One of the key texts on which our suspicion of the struggles for power is based is 2:12, where we find the prohibition to teach or to dominate the men (*anēr*). Although the Greek word *anēr* can also be translated as "husband," here, because it appears in the context of the community's liturgy, it would have to be understood as "male." It seems as though the problem has been raised by the male leaders of the community. The text, although directed toward the women of the community, focuses on rich women. The prohibition implies that these women are teaching in the church, which was common in the early Christian communities, but for some reason this exhortation demands stopping this practice. That is, the author does not want women to continue teaching. The motives can be linked to the problem of what the author considers to be teachings foreign to the gospel, which supposes that these women find these teachings appealing and are sharing them with other women, as we will see in the third chapter. We think, though, that above all, the prohibition of 2:12 is the result of the strong influence of these rich and powerful women over the whole community. The issue was that some women were well off, and, because of the patronage system (to which we will refer to below) were socially above the men. The "honor" of these women according to the parameters of Greco-Roman society was above both men and women of lesser means. The affirmation not to dominate or exercise authority is highly significant in this context. It does not refer to husbands, as we said above, but to men in general. By the tensions referred to in the text, we believe that the author has in mind particularly the male leaders of the community, elected by the assembly, with the imposition of hands by the elders (5:17-22).[15] The Greek verb *authentein* means "to control, to dominate, to compel, to influence in something, to act independently, to assume authority over, to usurp, etc."[16]

We find ourselves, then, with a struggle for power between the rich women who teach without being officially named and the male leadership. The author of the letter sends instructions to remove the rich women from leadership positions; but by writing the letter and speaking in generic terms, he unfortunately penalizes all women of all social conditions.

How is it possible that the rich women have achieved power within the community? For us in Latin America today, the answer is easy: it is an everyday occurrence in our Christian communities. Wealth and power easily open doors in all circles, not just in the secular world. People very often remain silent when favors (preferences, permissions, places, goods, etc.) are received by the rich on different occasions without much effort, just because of their social position. Many people even pay them tribute. The ancient world was not very different. The Letter of James criticizes the servile attitude when the brothers and sisters of the Christian community reserve the best places for the splendidly dressed rich who come to the assembly, while the poor dressed in rags are left behind and given the worst place (Jas. 2:1-4).

One explanation for the powerful influence of wealthy men and women in the early Christian communities is what is called the patronage system, which tied the relationships of those who had less with those who had more. This system is key for understanding the preeminence of certain women and certain men in this Ephesian community. Let us look at what it means.

The System of Patronage

The system of patronage, also called a system of benefactors, consisted of an exchange of relationships between those of unequal means. When a rich and powerful person gave a favor and protection to another person of an inferior status, a permanent relationship was established between patron and client. The patron gave what the other needed, and the one who received had to compensate in some way for the favor received. Generally, people repaid the favor, rewarding the persons who did the favor by praising their generosity, paying tribute to their honor or services and being loyal forever. Because honor was one of the fundamental values at that time, patrons needed praise in order to conserve their status and power in society. There was also a system of relationships between equals to do mutual favors; these were called friendship relations and did not fall into patron–client relationships.

Patronage was not limited to relations between people; it also took place between the rich and a city. For example, the rich made public donations to their city in the form of buildings, monuments, and food for the poor, as we will see below. Of course, the benefactors always wanted to be recognized and given the honor that their favors merited.

The patronage system was one of the essential pillars of the Roman social system. The cities, in order to support themselves and advance in the construction of theaters, baths, and monuments and to avoid discontent among the unemployed and the poor, needed patrons or benefactors who would also offer food and celebrations. Richard Horsley has come to the conclusion that, thanks to the patronage system, there were few internal rebellions against the Roman imperial government.[17]

The patronage system was present at all levels of Roman society, from the highest to the very lowest. The emperor, called Benefactor or Protector, centralized his power and controlled the senators and equestrians (two orders of the aristocracy) through the patronage system, offering favors to the wealthy of the aristocracy. These clients had to respond with loyalty so that the emperor's power was exercised through them. Likewise, the generals and governors sent by the emperor became patrons, and the local authorities, or decurions, became clients, obligated to give honor and loyalty to those sent from Rome.

In turn, the local authorities and local aristocracy of the cities did favors for those of lower rank, establishing the patronage relationship. The rich families of the provinces donated public buildings and subsidized celebrations, games, banquets, and the like, for which they were rewarded. Inscriptions in their honor, statues, letters of gratitude, effusive praise, votes for election as member of council, and so on show the obligatory response of those who benefited from the favor, such as associations,[18] rulers of the city, and the poor people in general, who sometimes also received food. The actions of these benefactors or patrons were called *euergesiai,* that is, good works.

This patronage system was present in all areas of life: in politics, business, and personal relationships. Even a philosopher or a writer might be obligated to become a client to a rich patron in order to survive. It would be almost impossible to have a rebellion against the imperial power because everyone except the indigent was compromised in some way as a client to a patron of superior rank. The patronage system was very effective for social control and constituted a strategy of social cohesion.[19]

Favors could be of any kind: intercession in a legal case; a recommendation in the political sphere; a loan for the gathering of the harvest, to buy land, or anything else; the concession of Roman citizenship, and so on. Patronage was present in personal and public relations. It was also present in the associations. One or more rich members would offer a sum of money for the maintenance of the association or would give banquets or other benefits. The members would then respond with banquets in his honor, or the honor of his family, or with inscriptions, statues, or votes to support his election to the board of directors.

Wealthy women also participated in this patronage system. They could be patrons of associations, of persons, and also of cities by giving donations to public works, such as baths, temples, or other buildings.

It is logical to suppose that the influence of this system, so common and familiar in all the Roman empire, was very strong in the Christian communities. For example, a man or woman head of a wealthy family who would offer his/her house to the community would be considered a patron and very probably expected to be recompensed in some way by the other members. And because the patronage system was contrary to the gospel's principles of equality, conflicts with rich men and women would not have been surprising. This situation can be seen in 1 Timothy 6:17-19.

THE WEALTHY SHOULD NOT EXPECT TO BE REWARDED FOR THEIR FAVORS

The Text: 1 Timothy 6:17-19

In 6:17-19 the author sends certain instructions for the wealthy members of the Christian community. Again, we insist that the instructions do not describe the way the wealthy are living but most likely the contrary. The instructions aim to correct or to show a desire for new conduct.

Let us look at the recommendations and their implications:

> [17] As for those who in the present age are rich, command them not to be haughty, or set their hopes on the uncertainty of riches, but rather on God who richly provides us with everything for our enjoyment. [18] They are to do good, to be rich in good works, generous, and ready to share, [19] thus storing up for themselves the treasure of a good foundation for the future, so they may take hold of the life that really is life.

The instructions are directed to the rich (*plousiois*), masculine plural, but this implicitly includes rich women, who were mentioned in 2:9. The expression "rich in the present age" refers to those who already have material goods in their Greco-Roman society. These, to be able to fit into the Christian community of Ephesus, must be distinct from those wealthy who follow the values of the imperial Roman society, that is, those customs that belong to the patronage system. The benefactors or patrons did good works in the cities or did favors to others, always expecting to be rewarded with honor or recognition as reciprocal payment for the favor or gift given. All this was done to consolidate their status and power. If they gave magnanimously, they did so to get more honor and recognition. In his work *Moralia*, Plutarch (ca. 50-120 C.E.) reproaches this attitude and affirms that this extravagance of the rich was a mask that really hid their love for money.[20] According to Reggie McReynolds Kidd, the author of 1 Timothy has in mind the behavior of the wealthy in the Christian community when he writes this exhortation. In a certain sense, the instructions to the rich believers are a criticism of the haughty and self-interested behavior of the rich in general, lovers of fame, money, and power.

The author proposes seven recommendations for the rich. In the first (v. 17a), he rejects arrogance or haughtiness. This is a characteristic of those who possess wealth and look down on everyone else. This is the first recommendation because the Christian community was made up of different social strata, with the majority living in poverty. Christians had inherited the values of humility and simplicity from the tradition of Jesus, so that there should not be members who believed they were superior to the rest. The second recommendation (v. 17b) is connected to the third (v. 18a), which has to do with hope placed in wealth and not in God. For the author, riches are uncertain, so to put hope in them is nonsense (see Luke 12:13-21). Our hope must be placed in God, because, unlike money, God does not defraud. This text is like a strong echo of Luke 16:13, which demands a decision between God and money (*mammon*). It must be recognized that God is the giver of all, and one must enjoy those gifts with rejoicing, not accumulate them with greed or squander them with the intention of raising oneself to a higher status or more recognition, because this is also "love of money," as Plutarch thought. The love of money, as has already been said by the author in 6:10, is the root of all evil.

The four following recommendations have to do with the sharing of solidarity: To do good (*agathoergein*) to others, to be rich in good works (*ploutein*), to be generous (*eumetadotous*) and to be in solidarity (*koinōnikous*). The emphasis on sharing and giving is obvious. This would be, for the author, the principal role of the rich; their task in the community is none other than to support the community economically. The author is probably referring to the solidarity of the rich with their poor brothers and sisters of the community, such as the abandoned widows (5:3 and 16b), which was the most important task of solidarity of the early church.

What is interesting in 1 Timothy 6:17-19 is the relationship of the rich to the patronage system.[21] Wealthy women and men will have their reward from God. To share with others is a good investment to be able to reach true life. In other words, the author, in a reasonable way, is saying to the rich that they are not to expect, because of their gifts and good works in the community, the submission of the members or the leaders. They should not expect to be given honor, recognition, or praise, as they were accustomed to receive in the meritocratic Greco-Roman society. They will receive their recompense from God, a reward that leads to true life, life that is authentic, integral, and in solidary. Thus, if the rich women and the well-to-do-men expected to assume prominent positions in the community simply because of their donations, the author forbids that. If someone wants to be an overseer, even though it would be a "noble task," that person must comply with certain requirements.[22]

The fact that the rich expected to be rewarded in some way by the Christian community could come from the existing custom in the so-called voluntary associations or clubs. We place the text in the context of the associations.

Associations and the Christian Community in 1 Timothy

In the Greco-Roman cities there existed the custom of forming groups based on common interest and meeting periodically.[23] The Romans used the Latin term *collegia* to refer to them. They were associations or brotherhoods; some were small, with about twelve members, and some grew to thirty. Very seldom would an association have more than forty members. In these associations, or clubs as some also call them, people in the city found a certain sense of belonging. They would meet to celebrate suppers or banquets, according to the social position of the association; to worship some god, offering sacrifices; to discuss some theme of common interest; to celebrate the funeral of one of their members. There were associations whose members had a common profession or employment, or who venerated a particular god. Besides a leader who directed the group, there was a treasurer to gather the monthly quotas to defray the costs of the association, such as festivals in honor of the patrons or benefactors, banquets, suppers, funerals, and the like. There was also a priest for the religious rituals or sacrifices. An association had its constitution or rules, and it was common for rich members to serve as patrons or benefactors, offering donations of their wealth to the association. They could also offer their houses for the meetings and pay the cost of the supper or banquet, or the animals offered to the gods. As a reward, the patrons or benefactors would receive special treatment; for example, the chief of the club would receive a double portion at the banquets.[24]

The authorities of the Roman empire felt a certain mistrust toward these associations because they considered them to be possible centers of conspiracies. It was for this reason, as John E. Stambaugh and David L. Balch point out, that the Roman authorities reduced the associations to three types.[25] One type was associations formed by the city's poor; these were called *collegia tenuiorum* (artisan associations). The poor members had legal permission to form an association; the main purpose was so that they would have a funeral when they died. Normally, the poor were buried in a common grave, lacking resources for a dignified ceremony. Therefore, the associations of this category fulfilled the primary function of offering a funeral and accompanying the dead in a procession to one of the tombs placed outside the city. The tomb was acquired by the association with a small monthly quota given by its members. The members also had to give an inscription fee to participate in the association. Another advantage of belonging to the association was attending the meetings, where members would eat together once a month and strengthen the bonds of friendship.

Another type of association was the *collegia sodalitia*, which had a religious function. These associations met to worship a particular god. The majority of these groups were formed by foreigners who wished to continue worshiping the god or gods of their ancestors.

The third type, the most prominent, was created for owners of certain types of businesses (shipping, transport, bakeries, carpentry, etc.). The majority of these types of *collegia*, above all the owners of ships, had sufficient money to offer the city monuments, buildings, or other economic services. As was true in all associations, the members established the criteria for membership and set the number of members. They also chose a god to whom to offer sacrifices.

The Jewish communities that met in synagogues and the Christians who met in houses were often confused with the *collegia sodalitia*, which were religious. The wealthy Gentile men and women were probably members of one of the professional associations and probably expected to be treated as patrons or benefactors in the Christian communities. These communities, heirs of the Jewish prophetic tradition, did not have this custom; in fact they said "do not let your left hand know what your right hand is doing," making it understood that solidarity with the poor is done in secret and from the heart and not to receive admiration and honor.

In sum, we believe, with Kidd, that this instruction from the author is criticizing the patronage system, which legitimated and consolidated social stratification and the subjugation of some by others. It is possible that the wealthy of that community thought it was normal that they would assume leadership without being responsible to anyone. In any case they were probably paying the expenses of the community. The elected leaders, with fewer resources but legitimately named, were possibly ignored by the rich. It is not by chance that the author encourages Timothy, the official carrier of the letter, saying, "Let no one despise your youth" (4:2). Moreover, the author exhorts Timothy not to accept any accusation against an elder except on the evidence of two or three (5:19), to do nothing on the basis of partiality or favoritism, not to hastily lay hands on anyone for leadership in the community without meditation (5:21-22), and to be sure that the elders who teach and preach well are paid double[26] (5:17). The texts make it clear that there are struggles for power within the community between the wealthy and the elders and other leaders named by the laying on of hands. It seems as if the wealthy are putting pressure on the young Timothy, because they think that since they are benefactors they have rights over the community and its leaders. That may be why the author of the letter three times encourages Timothy, who has no wealth or power so as to be treated as an equal by the rich of the community, to value his rights as a legitimate leader named through the laying on of hands (1:18; 4:14; 6:12).

But this does not finish the author's criticism of the rich. Let us look now at a text that joins these passages with "other teachings" and the idea of believing that godliness is a means of gain.

GODLINESS IS NOT A MEANS OF GAIN

The Text: 1 Timothy 6:3-10

The text (6:17-19) that we have just analyzed about the rich has been seen as out of context because of the apparent thematic contrast with the preceding verses (6:11-16), which contain wise advise for Timothy and conclude with a doxology.[27] Nevertheless, we believe that 6:17-20 forms an integral and coherent part of the chapter.[28] We now think, as do Countryman and Kidd, that the principal opponents are, in fact, the patrons of the community, especially the rich women who at the same time teach or associate with and support teachers who promote ideas contrary to those of the author of 1 Timothy. Thus, 6:17-19 is like a conclusion to the problem of wealth that began in 6:3-10 with an attack against those who love money. The following verses, 6:11-14, counsel Timothy to act in a radically different manner from those who love money and see godliness as a financial investment. The doxology of vv. 15-16 emphasizes that honor and power belong to God alone, the only sovereign.

For the author, the rich, who believe themselves experts in teaching and want to impose that teaching on the community, are not teaching with godliness. Even worse, they believe that godliness is a means to gain, in the sense of status, honor, and power. Let us look at the text:

> [6:3] Whoever teaches otherwise and does not agree with the sound words of our Lord Jesus Christ and the teaching that is in accord with godliness, [4] is conceited, understanding nothing, and has morbid craving for controversy and for disputes about words. From these come envy, dissension, slander, base suspicions, [5] and wrangling among those who are depraved in mind and bereft of the truth, imagining that godliness is a means of gain. [6] Of course, there is great gain in godliness combined with contentment; [7] for we brought nothing into the world, so that we can take nothing out of it; [8] but if we have food and clothing, we will be content with these. [9] But those who want to be rich fall into temptation and are trapped by many senseless and harmful desires that plunge people into ruin and destruction. [10] For the love of money is the root of all kinds of evil, and in their eagerness to be rich some have wandered away from the faith and pierced themselves with many pains.

This passage is very intriguing; it mixes love of money, godliness, and other teachings. The composition is interesting because it seems as if vv. 3, 5b-6, and 10 form a circle in which the three themes are united. Verse 3 alludes to certain persons who teach a message different from "the sound words of our Lord Jesus Christ and the teaching that is in accordance with godliness." Verse 5b affirms that these people believe that "godliness is a means of gain." And v. 10 repeats the saying that the root of all evil is the love of money, and it warns those who vehemently (*oregomenoi*) covet or desire riches that they will not only wander away from the faith but cause pain to themselves.

Verses 3 and 10 are united explicitly by the theme of "other teachings" (v. 3) and straying from the faith (v. 10). The diversion from the faith would mean distancing from the sayings or teachings (*logois*)[29] of Jesus and moving closer to another kind of teaching (v. 3). We know that in the Gospels there is a radical critique of those who love wealth; the Gospels even demand deciding between God and wealth (Matt. 6:24). Wealth was considered an idol if all hope is put there. The saying "The root of all evil is the love of money" was a well-known maxim at that time. Bion, for example, said that "the love of money was the city-mother of all evil."[30] The thoughts about wealth in antiquity were not the same as today; accumulation was seen as wrong, the same as usury and greed. The wealthy should give a good part of their money to benefit the city, in the distribution of food for the population or in entertainment when it was necessary. The rich who were stingy or in love with money were criticized by the philosophers of that time. Today, everything is geared to the maximization of profits; everything is calculated to facilitate our own enrichment, without thought for the future well-being of the poor. It was not like this in antiquity; the Gospels criticize the attitude of love of money, as did the Greco-Roman writers. The difference between the two is that the Gospel invites us to love God and to be in solidarity with our neighbor freely, and the Greco-Roman values promote the love of honor, status, and power as a reward for those who give generously. It is because of this that the author of 1 Timothy exhorts the rich (6:18) to give generously, and their reward will be life that is really life, since now and forever power and honor are for God alone (6:16). Let us look in detail at the relation between these verses, and we will be surprised that these are not just a simple series of warnings or sayings without coherence, as some think.

Money, Godliness, and Other Teachings

1 Timothy 6:3 affirms that the words or sayings of Jesus are sound and are in accord with godliness (*eusebeia*), the way to be Christian. This is contrasted with v. 10, in which love of money is not only different from the teaching of Jesus, but is a sickness that separates us from sincere faith and causes much suffering. Those who desire and love money cannot act with godliness; that is to say, they cannot manifest coherent behavior as followers of Jesus Christ.

Verses 5-8, which form the center of the passage, perfectly join with vv. 3 and 10. Those who "teach otherwise" than the words of Jesus Christ and godliness (v. 3), according to the author, have a corrupted mind and are deprived of the truth; they think that godliness means gain, a way to make money, a source of economic gain (*porismon*) (v. 5). The relation with v. 3 lies in that they are deprived of, or have denied themselves (*apesterēmenon*), the truth of the Gospel (2:5). They are the ones who are teaching something different from the words of Jesus and the teachings of godliness. The author is clear that godliness is only advantageous (v. 6) if we live according to the words of Jesus, that is, with actions and attitudes of contentment (*autarkeias*) with what we have, in the sense of not having an eagerness for more money and profit. There is no need to accumulate money and goods when we have that which is necessary, such as food and clothing (v. 8). It is useless to accumulate, for we brought nothing into the world and have no needs after we die (v. 8). Those who live according to the "truth of the Gospel" will have a more fulfilling life than those living with an accumulation of economic goods. The relation of vv. 5-8 with v. 10 is climactic: the root of all evil is the love of money, and for that reason it is a true heresy to make godliness a transaction. It is against the words of Jesus and true godliness.

We have seen a harmonious circle in which the most important points are 6:3, 5-8, and 10. Now we need to examine the intermediate verses, 4 and 9. Verse 4 speaks negatively of those persons who teach something different from the words of Jesus and describes the damaging consequences of that behavior. Verse 9 describes the damaging consequences for those who want to be rich. If we relate those two texts, we find that, for the author, those who teach something different from the words of Jesus Christ are those who want to be rich or to keep their wealth (*ploutein*).[31] These, according to v. 4, are vain, understanding nothing, having a morbid craving for controversy and useless disputes. For the author of the letter, this is harmful, a sickness that produces envy, discord, slander, and base suspicions. Their minds have been corrupted and have gone so far from the truth of the Gospel that they believe that godliness or Christian piety is a transaction. But the author speaks about the consequences the rich will suffer for keeping their wealth. According to human experience, those persons fall into temptation, greedy and harmful desires that plunge them into ruin and destruction (v. 9). That is why the author reminds them that the love of money is the source of all evil. How is it possible to believe that godliness is a source for making money? This is the great heresy for the author.

Let us look at the concentric structure of this passage:

  A Some are teaching something different from the sound words of Jesus Christ and godliness (v. 3).

      B Those who are vain, understanding nothing, dedicate themselves to useless discussions, leading to envy, dissension, slander, discord, and base suspicions (v. 4).

         C They have left the truth and believe that godliness is gain (v. 5).

         C' Godliness is great gain if one lives with contentment with that which one has (vv. 6-8).

      B' Those who want to be rich or hang onto their wealth are trapped in dangerous desires and fall into ruin and destruction (v. 9).

  A' The root of all evil is the love of money; those who covet it or let themselves be attracted by it wander away from the faith and cause themselves much pain (v. 10).

Verses 6-8 merit a clarification. These texts stand out because of being used in telling people that they should be happy with what they have, that is, be satisfied with the basic necessities such as food and clothing. We know that these texts have been taken out of context to discourage or combat peoples' popular struggles for better salaries, housing, education, and other things that are necessary for a dignified life. This is a manipulation of the text. When we read these verses, we have to understand that when the author says that there is great gain in godliness combined with "contentment," he uses the Greek word *autarkeias,* which literally means "self-sufficiency." What is fundamental here is that the author puts *autarkeias* in opposition to the love of money and the desire to accumulate wealth, because these lead to ruin and unhappiness. He recommends as more beneficial being content with what one possesses, having the basic needs covered, rather than being eager to accumulate goods. The same critique and counsel appear in Ecclesiastes 5:12-14 and also in Proverbs 30:8. Therefore, this text cannot be taken out of context to discourage the aspirations of the poor to have a wage that will support with dignity their life and that of their family.

To summarize, in 6:3-10 we find that in the community to which this letter is directed some wealthy people, or persons who want to become wealthy, teach something other than the sound words of Jesus Christ. They do not act with godliness: on the contrary, they are vain and have left the truth of the Gospel, supposing that godliness is a transaction, and are eager to accumulate more than what is necessary for self-sufficiency, which leads to ruin and destruction. They have forgotten that the root of all evil is the love of money and run the risk of not only straying away from the faith but causing much suffering to themselves.

These could be the rich members of the Christian community, whom Timothy should exhort not to puff up with pride, but to share generously without rewards, such as glory or power on the earth (6:17-19). Or they could be persons who are not rich but want to become rich. This is a possibility; we noted that the present infinitive of the Greek *ploutein* ("to enrich oneself," "to be rich") allows that (see n. 31). The Letter of James makes a distinction between the rich landowners (Jas. 5:1-6) and persons who plot to do business so they can make money. In this case, the author of 1 Timothy would attack those who want to become rich more than those who are already rich. Because of the context, however, we are inclined to agree with Kidd that it deals with the persons who are already rich and remain tied to their wealth.[32]

The author recommends to Timothy that he flee from these practices and attitudes and look for other values, such as justice, godliness, faith, and love. He encourages Timothy to be strong against this group of people who teach something else and want to impose it because of their status and wealth. For the author, Timothy must resist and remain faithful as did Jesus before Pilate (6:11-15). This last phrase is surprising. He uses the figure of Jesus when confronted with the power of Pontius Pilate before being condemned to be crucified. Pilate was a Roman procurator of the equestrian order, which was in charge of the occupation forces that had total control over the Judean province. This example indicates that the situation was very difficult for Timothy to have to confront the power of the benefactors or patrons.

The Wealthy, Godliness, and Struggles for Power

Now let us ask ourselves about the relationship of these texts to the struggles for power in the community that we have referred to in this chapter. At first impression, it seems as if there is not much relation; however, when we consider "other teachings" with "the wealthy" we indirectly find the idea of struggle in relation to leadership. Key terms are "other teaching," "godliness" (piety), and "love of money." We considered these words together above and observed that, for the author, those who love money are the same ones who teach otherwise. If they have been criticized for teaching otherwise, it means that they are already doing it, or are struggling to do so. According to the author, they are conceited or have become extremely arrogant (*tetyphō-tai*), and he tries to disqualify them by saying that they understand nothing and like to pass their time in arguing over the meaning of words (*logomachias*), becoming involved in a useless war of words. Although we have to distinguish between the rhetorical discourse of the author and reality, there is no doubt that there is in these opponents a sense of superiority over the rest of the community, including the leaders. This sense of superiority is because they are the benefactors or patrons who economically support the community and have sufficient time to dedicate themselves to lucubrate their arguments on genealogies and myths. According to the author, their behavior does not correspond to godliness or the modest and simple religiosity inherited from Jesus and Paul. Their godliness is something else, and worse, it is related to gain. But what does godliness (*eusebeia*) mean in 1 Timothy?

1 Timothy has a preference for this term, differing from the other writers of the New Testament. Some think that 1 Timothy uses the term "godliness" (*eusebeia*) in the same sense that it was used outside the circle of Christians. "Godliness" was a term frequently used in the time in which the epistle was written. For the Romans "it meant to scrupulously respect the common tradition, be it a religious law, an order coming from religious authorities or simply a tradition conserved by the pontiffs."[33] It generally dealt with laws and orders that had to be respected, such as cultic rituals. The ungodly would then be "those that violate ritual prescriptions." In this way ungodliness and unclean correspond, as do godliness and purity.[34]

Reading the letter carefully, however, it seems that the sense of godliness in 1 Timothy is different. The influence of the Hebrew Bible is obvious. For the author, *eusebeia* is more than the respectful practice of cultic traditions; it is the way to live the Christian life, in which the commitment to God is reflected in the practice of everyday life. The difficulty will lie in the understanding that one has of the practice of daily life before God and the cultural values assumed in the patriarchal household. We will see this in the second chapter, but we won't go ahead now: we will continue analyzing the term "godliness" (*eusebeia*). The word unites the fear of God with the knowledge of God and with the concrete and visible practice that this knowledge must reveal. An unjust practice, for example, reveals a false knowledge of God and a lack of the fear of God. For this reason, the author can speak against other teachings that differ from the words of Jesus, whose words conform to godliness (6:3). Thus, when some think that godliness is a means of gain, they do not reveal real knowledge of God nor do they fear God. "They are conceited . . ." says the author of 1 Timothy.

Now we will try to respond to a more difficult question: Why do the rich or those who want to become rich believe that godliness is a source of gain?

Some think that this has to do with persons who charged for their teachings (for the author, false teachings). If that were the case, these persons would not be rich but would have the ambition to be rich, and for them it would be easy to please the rich who paid for the teachings. In this case it would deal above all with the rich women, because they would be more interested in teachings that reject marriage (4:3). The author would then criticize this attitude in those who wanted to become rich, as well as those who were rich. This proposal is consistent with the text. It would also shed light on the issue of double remuneration to the elders especially because they preach and teach (for the author) correct teachings. Here the struggle is between those who teach "other teachings" ("different from the sound teachings of Jesus") and charge for it, and the elders who should be paid double for their eagerness for good preaching and teaching. In any case, those who want to enrich themselves as well as those who are already rich and lovers of money should not form part of the leadership as either *episkopoi* or deacons, according to the qualities demanded in 3:3 and 3:8. They must be disinterested in money and enemies of illicit gain.

Now then, if we believe that the persons mentioned in 6:3-10 are the rich, we will have to look for another answer to this difficult question. The rich, for the author, have a false godliness; but why do they think that godliness is a means of gain? We do not find a satisfactory solution to this question. One of the answers could be that the rich, upon demonstrating godliness—in the religious sense, devoted and generous with their money—believed that they would receive honor and fame, as they would have in the patronage system. This reward from the clients (in this case the other members of the community) would reinforce the status and power of patrons. It could be that these rich persons would have in mind the Roman meaning of "godliness," which meant scrupulously following the rituals so as to find favor with the gods and honor from the religious authorities and their fellow citizens.

This last manner of understanding godliness as a means of

gain is not foreign to our context of today's Latin America. There are television programs and large churches, driven by the so-called prosperity theology, in which it is demanded that the people make investments through offerings and donations in order to receive more money from God and to prosper economically. For the author of 1 Timothy this conception of godliness is a heresy, in that it does not follow the tradition of Jesus and the Hebrew Scriptures.

Going back to the wealthy in the Christian community of Ephesus, if godliness is a means of gain, then those who were rich would try to occupy spaces for leadership to obtain more power and status. We find, then, that there are struggles for power to occupy leadership positions in the Christian community.

As we have been able to observe, the position of the author is not a simple one. On the one hand, his radical attitude to women is disconcerting; on the other hand, we see an attractive position with regard to his critique of those who look for power because of their wealth and prestige. The rejection of controversy and disputes that oppose the simplicity of the words of the Gospel is also suggestive for our popular reading of the Bible. What is difficult to accept is the generalization of the exclusion of women, the assimilation of the values of the patriarchal household at the time of the Roman empire, and the incapacity to enter into dialogue with new ideas. We will take up these difficult issues in the next chapters. Let us look at the text now from the perspective of the patriarchal household and power relations between the genders.

2

The Patriarchal Household and
Power Relations between Genders

In the first chapter we analyzed the problem of the wealthy in
the Christian community of 1 Timothy at the end of the first
century or the beginning of the second century. We have seen
how the patronage system caused tensions within the community, especially with the rich women who asserted their authority
because of their power, wealth, and status. We will now analyze
the letter from the perspective of gender. That is to say, we will
now concentrate on those texts in which we can see the power
relations between men and women. To do that, we will also try
to reconstruct the setting of the cultural values of the patriarchal
society of the Roman empire.

This is not an easy task, because gender and social position
were interwoven with the persons who enter the scene. In
1 Timothy 5:1-16, for example, we find poor widows and well-
to-do widows as well as patriarchal instructions to resolve
economic and gender conflicts. In 3:1-7, which speaks of the
qualities of those who aspire to the position of supervisor in the
leadership of the ecclesial community, we find the exclusion of
women, rich and poor, through the imposition of certain qualities assigned to male heads of the family (*patresfamilias*); and
2:8-15 reflects the imposition of patriarchal values that did not
permit women to teach and a patriarchal lecture in which women
are depicted as inferior, not qualified to teach and created only
to be mothers.

In this chapter we will analyze 2:8-14 and 5:3-16 from the
perspective of gender, inserting information about the context
of the ancient patriarchal society, and, as we have already said,
trying to reconstruct the tense situation of the Christian com-

munity of Ephesus. We will begin with the sociocultural context. To be able to understand the letter, it is fundamental to know something about the concepts of family, household, honor, and shame.

THE CULTURAL BACKGROUND OF THE GRECO-ROMAN IMPERIAL PATRIARCHAL SOCIETY

The Family in the Empire

For the Greeks and Romans, the family was an essential element of the society. It involved the patriarchal family, in which the father, head of the household and owner of the house, was called *paterfamilias.* He was considered the landowner and was at the same time responsible for his wife, for his children, and frequently for his grandchildren and great grandchildren who still lived under the same roof. Those who had to submit to him were not only his own blood family but all who lived in his house: slaves, if he had any; freedmen, who legally were still tied to the head of the household; and other persons, for example, those who because of favors received from the owner of the household remained tied to him for the return of the favors.[1] As can be seen, the term *familia* in antiquity covers not only family relationships but also all those who were dependent on and subordinated to the head of the household.

Marriage and procreation were fundamental to the patriarchal society. Carolyn Osiek and David Balch show that marriage was a social contract between two families for legitimate reproduction and the legal transmission of property.[2]

At the beginning of the first century, the emperor Augustus promulgated a law that obliged women to follow the patterns of the patriarchal household, to marry and have children. He also imposed strong sanctions against adultery committed by women.[3] The emperor was concerned that the aristocracy might not reproduce. Besides that, the governing class and the males of the aristocracy, with their imperial ideology, were afraid that gender roles might be inverted as well as the roles of others who were subordinated to the owner of the household, such as children and slaves. For the aristocracy, a change in the patriarchal household would mean chaos. Greek and Roman thinkers such as Cicero, Seneca, Tacitus, Dionysius, and others repeated the vertical concepts of Aristotle with respect to the family, and, what is even more interesting, they compared the city government with the family. For them, both governments were the same. The king was like the *paterfamilias*: he should watch over and protect his subordinates and make them obey, as the father did in his household with his subordinates. The subordinates must obey and submit to the king and the city (or imperial) authorities as the dependents of the patriarchal family submitted to the father. The patriarchal household values were intrinsically united to the values of society. For this reason it is called a patriarchal society. Elisabeth Schüssler Fiorenza rightly prefers to refer to this social setting as "patrikyriarchal," adding the Greek term *kyrios,* meaning "Lord."[4]

This does not mean that there were not rich women, owners of households, who demanded submission of their children, slaves, and persons who had received favors from them. This was common in the case of rich widows or rich divorced women who, because of their wealth, power, and status, received honors from their dependents and clients.[5] The patriarchal household was the ideal of the masculine and imperial or governmental ideology. In reality, wealthy women who did not submit opposed these values, as did poor women, who had to work with their husbands or alone in order to survive.

According to ancient extrabiblical documents, the participation of women in public activities in the city was ambiguous and depended not only on their gender but also on their wealth and status. Rich women could attend the theater, but they sat apart; they could also attend banquets with their husbands, but had to leave when the *symposion* began. That was a time to drink, have philosophical discussions or simple conversations, and engage in erotic activities.[6] These well-to-do women could also participate in worship activities, whether to the emperor or to another god or goddess, in the city or in the house, but always with marginal roles and under the orders of the men in charge. It was understood that poor women, as well as their husbands, were excluded from these social activities.

The Domestic Codes

Various texts in 1 Timothy mention the behavior of the household members: the father, the wife, the children, and the slaves. These four groups have a place and a social role to fulfill according to the ideal of the patriarchal household. In 2:11-12, the author orders women to learn in silence and not to dominate the men. Even though these texts do not necessarily refer to husband and wife, the position each one should have in society, especially the role of submission of the woman in the household, is implicit. In 3:4 one of the qualities of the supervisor (*episkopos*) of the Christian community is that "he must manage his own household well, keeping his children submissive and respectful (*semnotētos*) in every way." In 6:1-2 slaves are told to respect their masters (believers or not). The mention of these three groups of distinct members of the household, with one being superior to the other, reflects what are commonly known as "domestic codes," because they refer to the administration of the household.[7] In this way, the man, owner of the household, is the husband, father, and master to whom all must pay respect and submit.

According to some scholars, these codes go back to Aristotle (384-322 B.C.E.), who in his work *Politics* speaks of the administration of the household, because the state is made up of family units. The parts of the family are expressed in pairs, beginning with master and slave, followed by husband and wife, concluding with father and children. Afterward, he continues his discourse basing the authority and superiority in the master, husband, and father over the slave and the rest of the household members. He also adds a fourth element to the domestic economy, namely "the art of amassing a fortune."[8]

After Aristotle, many philosophers and thinkers of antiquity continued transmitting the same idea, using similar schemes, sometimes with fixed and stereotypical forms and other times with some variants. But deep down the superiority and authority of the male as *paterfamilias* was always affirmed. For the ancient writers the authority and the subordination of the household and the city were the same. To administer the household well was a patriotic duty.[9] Any kind of inversion in the order of the household authority meant subversion, even a catastrophe, for the order of the city.

In the minds of these thinkers was the image of rich aristocratic families, since those who constituted legally formed families were free citizens and those who had houses and slaves were usually the wealthy. But, as we affirmed earlier, the ideal was not limited to the wealthy households. Patriarchal ideology penetrated the whole of society and all social sectors. Even when the lower sectors were unable to reach the ideal because of their condition, it was assumed to be natural and logical. We see in inscriptions with epitaphs of people who were not from the elite but for some reason (commercial or another reason) had sufficient money to be able to dedicate an epitaph to a loved woman, that the praises of a mother or a wife are imbued with patriarchal ideology.

In Roman imperial times the comportment of women of the Roman elite and also those of the governing classes of the provinces changed considerably with respect to the ideal woman according to tradition. The *paterfamilias* lost power, and the women of high society achieved much liberty of movement outside the household and within marriage. They controlled properties, and they could divorce, attend banquets and public events, and be public figures, at least as city benefactors with titles of honor. Patriarchal ideals clashed with reality.[10] The Julian law of the emperor Augustus with respect to marriage and children, the satires of Juvenal and Martial about Roman matrons and their dominion, plus the continuous traditional affirmations of the majority of thinkers (including Neoplatonists, Peripatetics, Stoics, Epicureans, Hellenist Jews, and Pythagoreans) with respect to the submissive behavior of women reflect their response of rejecting women's behavior that did not conform to the domestic codes and to women's position in the patriarchal society.

The Houses Where Families Lived

Archaeological excavations have allowed us to know about the houses of the wealthy as well as the apartment buildings called *insulae,* commonly constructed for persons of modest resources.

Generally books on the ancient urban environment dedicate many pages to the houses (*domus* in Latin; *oikoi* in Greek) of the rich, which have been better preserved. Nevertheless, centering so much on these houses runs the risk of losing the perspective of the contours of the whole city. The majority of the population (between 90 and 95 percent) were not members of the elite. Many of them lived in very crowded conditions in the miserable rooms of the *insulae*, which often did not have open spaces in their interior. Osiek and Balch comment, "The majority of the dwellers lived crowded in small, dark and poorly ventilated buildings, where there was neither privacy nor adequate hygiene and as a consequence the propagation of sickness was inevitable."[11] The high rate of infant mortality and reduced life expectancy at the time in which the First Letter to Timothy was written were not unusual. We also have to realize that part of the population did not have sufficient money even to pay rent and they had to sleep mainly around public buildings.[12]

As the demarcation of poor neighborhoods and the city center reflected the social stratification,[13] the homes also reflected the ideology of the dominant patriarchal class. It was imposed with greater force in the households of the wealthy and by governments or male thinkers in their discourses and writings. In fact, as Osiek and Balch say, "One of the key functions of the wealthy households was to reinforce social status and the difference . . . The architecture separated slaves from property owners and dinning rooms from kitchens."[14] They add that the household property owners had enormous power over all who lived under their roof.[15]

In Ephesus, the city where the community of 1 Timothy was located, archaeologists have found various houses of the wealthy built on the hill. The mosaics on the floors, as well as the ampleness of the perimeter, reflect the status of rich persons. It is possible that they had two or three floors. Since in the first floor there were signs of an interior garden (*peristilo*), a room where business was attended (*tablinum*) and another that could have been a multi-use room (*oecus*), it is possible that the bedrooms were on a second floor. Some of the houses in that city had a hot water system for the different rooms of the house besides having running water for baths, latrines, and the kitchen. The majority of the city's inhabitants used the city's baths and latrines and bought their food from shops on the street.

In front of these houses, before coming to the hill, were two blocks of two-story apartments (*insulae*) in which were a series of shops on the first floor and rooms for living on the second. The shops faced the street. These apartments were for persons with fewer resources, possibly the owners of the small stores that faced the street. They could also have been rooms rented to poor families who crowded together. In other cities similar buildings of apartments (*insulae*) have been found in which the rooms, one or two small and dark, were on the back side or on the second floor of the small stores.[16] Not all the *insulae* were for poor families, however. In highly populated cities such as Ostia and Rome there were *insulae* with more rooms, with even four to seven rooms in an apartment, with windows facing the street or the interior patio.[17] Except in a few cases, the *insulae* generally did not have kitchens, latrines, or baths.

The Cultural Values of Honor and Shame

Honor and shame, two values intimately related to the family and the household, were "foundational concepts of the first century."[18] In moral instructions or advice it was always specified what was honorable or what was not. Everyone's comportment was measured by these two concepts, which showed what people considered to be acceptable or reproachable. Whoever acted contrary to the customs valued by society suffered shame, so that the behavior of persons, families, and even communities was marked by the attention paid by others to them, according to the code of honor and shame.

Although it seems strange, these concepts were differentiated by gender in the patriarchal culture. The honor of women was not the same as that of men, and almost always it was related to their sexual behavior. If a woman refused an indecent invitation, such as to have an adulterous relationship, she conserved her honor; however, if she accepted, it became a shame for her and her household. The honor of a man consisted in defending his social status and the sexual virtue of the women in his family.

Honor for a woman was to maintain her virginity before marrying and to be faithful after marriage.[19] So much so, that to remain a widow and never to marry again so as to be faithful to her husband was one of the highest virtues for women.

The men of the household paid great attention to the sexual conduct of their women, because for them "women had a dangerous ability to bring shame to their families (especially to their male family members), through their sexual conduct."[20] That is the reason the ancient writings insist that a woman should stay in the house—this was her space and dominion—and participate as little as possible in public activities. Honor could be attained by status, power, and wealth, and by having a lifestyle designated as honorable according to the values of society.

The Patriarchal Household as an Ideal for the Concept of Family

It is important to underline that when we speak of household (*oikos*) in antiquity, we are not only referring to the place or building but also to the family and the conduct of the family in the household. The ideal of family—and here we have to underline *ideal*—was that the wife, the children, and the slaves if there were slaves—that is, all of the dependents of the head (man)—submitted in obedience to him, because he was the husband, the father, and the master. The space reserved for women was in the house. This was the ideal that may have existed in the ancient Greek and Roman households in the times of the Republic. By the middle of the Hellenistic period, however, there had already been generated a change in that the *paterfamilias* had lost certain power in his household and women had reached a certain level of independence.[21] Thus, in the Roman empire the patriarchal household only remained as an ideal of the male and governing elite, filled with nostalgia and discontent in the face of contrary conduct of women, especially wealthy women. On the other hand, as has always been said, the ideal conduct within the household was associated more with the elite than with those who did not belong to it. The construction of houses for the rich could have favored this ideal conduct for the patriarchal family in the wealthy citizen class. Women could stay in the spaces assigned to them,[22] but they did not do so. Moreover, in the *insulae*, without latrines or kitchens, women were obligated to use public space—not because they rebelled but because of need. In the small rooms of the apartments of the poor *insulae* there was barely room for a father, mother, and two or three children. Nevertheless, we would have to realize that, if the family had a small shop on the first floor, the owner could have one or two slaves who would live in the workshop or store itself.

Besides, neither non-citizens nor slaves could legally marry. The so called domestic codes, that required obedience and sub-mission to the *paterfamilias* by the wife, children, and slaves, were an ideal almost impossible to strictly follow, be it for social and legal changes in the society with respect to women or con-ditions of the lower classes, who were the majority of the inhab-itants of the city. The patriarchal ideal was one thing, the social reality was another.

Nevertheless, it is important to take into account that those domestic codes or norms did not go out of existence; on the con-trary, they were internalized also by the non-elite,[23] even by the poor. The codes always appeared as profound cultural values and as a model to follow, according to the moral or apologetical discourse. The codes continued to be a force which, even with-out a corresponding practice, served to restrict and crush aspi-rations of equality between family members. We will see later how in the First Letter to Timothy these values were affirmed and applied to all the families of different social strata.

For our study it is important to ask ourselves, when speaking of the household and domestic codes, if these codes really per-tain only to the rich who have houses or mansions (*oikos/domus*) or if they could also refer to people who lived in *insulae* for well-off persons,[24] as well as those who lived in *insulae* that had one or two rooms. The majority of the commentaries and books that deal with the theme of domestic administration refer only to the houses of the rich. This is because the literature that deals with this question refers only to the wealthy. Nevertheless, taking into account the interiorization of patriarchal values and the existence of families that had small businesses and workshops in which the father, mother, children, and maybe one or two slaves worked, it is logical to think of an administration and patriarchal relationships between those members in which the domestic codes were also applied. This point is important because, as we will see in 3:1-7, certain qualities required of the supervisor will be those that have to do with the administration of his household. If we affirm that only the rich administer a household, the requirements of the supervisors could be filled only by the wealthy members of the community, which would be a contradiction with respect to the author's confrontation with the rich, according to our interpretation.

Let us now analyze the texts against the background of a patriarchal culture as we have described it in reference to the family, the household, and the values of honor and shame in antiquity. We will begin by studying again 1 Timothy 2:8-15, but now from the perspective of gender.

AGAINST WOMEN WHO TEACH AND HAVE AUTHORITY OVER MEN

The Text: 1 Timothy 2:8-12

> [8] I desire, then, that in every place the men should pray, lifting up holy hands without anger or argument; [9] also that the women should dress themselves modestly and decently in suitable clothing, not with their hair braided, or with gold, pearls, or expensive clothes, [10] but with good works, as is proper for women who profess reverence for God. [11] Let women learn in silence with full submission. [12] I permit no woman to teach or have authority over a man; she is to keep silent.

The context of the instruction, as we said in the first chapter, is the liturgical assembly or the Christian community, in which the men should pray with hands raised and the women should not dress in an ostentatious manner. That is what most of the commentaries on the letter say. If that is so, then it deals with an assembly where men and women actively participated in prayer,[25] but because of the struggles for power the author wanted to eliminate the participation of women in the teaching. To teach (*didaskalein*) could here be a technical term meaning to teach that which is official or the tradition.[26] Chapter 3 of the letter, where the qualities of supervisor are indicated, where men are assigned, also seems to reinforce the context of the community. However, it could be that vv. 11 and 12 of chapter 2 also applied to women outside the context of the Christian community. The text gives the impression that the author wants submissive and resigned conduct, rather than the exercise of teaching and author- ity over men, to be applied also in the daily life of women.[27]

In chapter 1 above, we saw that the author deemed the pres- ence of rich women to be threatening, because they probably tried to dominate the rest of the members, including the official leadership, because of their wealth, status, and power. The text, because it is situated within the first instructions and written in a negative tone, indicates that there was a problem with this kind of woman. The different instruction for men and women is notable (v. 8), as we saw in the previous chapter. However, the main point of the letter is not in this conflictive situation, which probably involved only a small number of women benefactors or patrons. What is an issue, however, is the author's instruction on how to resolve the problem. Instead of resolving it in a non- authoritarian manner, he turns to the patriarchal ideology of those times—not only to call attention to the rich women caus- ing the problem, but to subjugate all the women, because patri- archal ideology is directed to all women, regardless of their social class.

To tell women how they should dress, even though here it is to avoid the contrast of the clothing worn by the rich and the poor of the assembly, is part of patriarchal ideology. The terms "decently," "modestly," "restraint," and "discretion," for exam- ple, in spite of the fact that the author contrasts them with osten- tatious hairdos, jewels, and costly clothing, still reflect the values that patriarchal society assigns to the feminine gender. By apply- ing to women the terms *aidous* ("discretion, modesty") and *sōphrosynēs* ("self-control, restraint"), the author causes the reader to think of "chastity," sexual purity. It is because patriar- chal ideology has associated women, throughout history, with sex and temptation. Shame is for women who dress with insolence and liberty. That is why, as we have seen, the men of the household—fathers, brothers, uncles, grandfathers—had the task of controlling the women so they would not be sexually provocative and damage the family's honor.

So the author of the letter gives instructions that the rich women not use jewels and expensive clothing in order to reduce the social inequality within the Christian community,[28] but at the same time the patriarchal ideology tells women how they should dress, using terms with connotations associated with chastity. For our reading of the Bible, what is important is to contrast the ostentatious with what is modest and simple, not with chastity. The problem is not the women's sexual provocation, but the ostentation of some of the wealthy women of the community.

If we do not show the real contrast, which is simplicity versus ostentation, the ambiguity of v. 9a leads some interpreters to assume uncritically certain values assigned to women in keeping with their feminine gender. That is why some commentators read here an instruction directed to ornamentation in the women's finery, in the sense that they should not dress in a flirtatious manner, but chastely:

> Knowing that the dress and ornamentation was an area of preoccupation for women, and that there is danger in falling into insolence and indiscretion, Paul focuses on this point in his advice and instruction to the women when referring to their manner of dressing.[29]

In this comment George W. Knight III forgets that men in antiquity as well as today like to preoccupy themselves with how they dress and flirt with women. Jerome D. Quinn and William C. Wacker translate *kosmein* as "to make oneself attractive,"[30] adding that it is oriented to the feminine role assigned by culture, and that if *kosmein* ("to adorn oneself") referred to men, it certainly would not have been translated "to make oneself attractive."

We note, then, two problems in 2:9: the text itself and the interpretations of the text. In both, the ideology of patriarchal society is present in assigning virtues in accord with gender. The concepts of family, household, honor, and shame have not varied much in the essentials. Our patriarchal culture today has deep roots in the Greco-Roman culture, the mother of Western culture.

Verse 10 continues the exhortation on clothing, now in a metaphoric sense. If v. 9 contrasted simplicity with ostentation, now the ostentation is contrasted with good works. The author underlines that in the end what is basic is that appearances are not important. In fact, to dress with simplicity is not a virtue in itself; it is the way humble persons in the community normally dress. Most important are good works. To profess reverence for God (*eusebeia*) means that women give testimony of their spirituality, their manner of being, as followers of Jesus. Godliness, *eusebeia*, is not a transaction, as some of the community thought (6:5), even if it is true that costly clothing gives status and power. *Eusebeia* is a spirituality oriented toward the words of Jesus (6:3), and it is reflected in the practice of good works.[31] Further on we will specify what "good works" meant for the author.

In chapter 1 we saw that in 2:11-12 the mandates that women should learn in silence with full submission and should not teach or have authority over men come out of the context of struggles for power. That probably means that some rich women took on positions of leadership simply because of their donations to the Christian community. Now, analyzing the texts from the perspective of gender, we see that the author tries to resolve the problem by going back to the domestic codes of patriarchal ideology. Instead of asking his delegate Timothy to discuss the model of leadership in terms of the "democratic" principles inherited from Jesus, in which the criterion of social condition would favor the poor, independent of gender, the author adopts the values of Greco-Roman patriarchal society, excluding women from teaching and obligating them to keep quiet and to learn.

Verses 11 and 12 bring us to the problem of other teachings and theologies considered heresies by the author, and, as it is probably these same women who hold those teachings, the text also tries to resolve that problem by going back to the traditional ideas about women's comportment in the household and society. The terms "to learn" (*manthaneto*) and "to teach" (*didaskein*) in the polemical context of other teachings and on the assumption that the women adopted the "other teachings" imply that the women teach without knowledge and therefore should learn in submission and silence—that is, without debating, questioning, or giving their opinion. In sum, the traditional ideas present in the domestic codes of patriarchal ideology, which exclude all women from teaching and leadership, are used by the author to resolve a circumstantial problem: some rich women dominated the community and probably taught something that the author did not like.

Some of the later writings of the New Testament, such as Ephesians, Colossians, and 1 Peter, repeat, although with certain variations of reciprocity, the traditional domestic codes reflecting the dominant ideal of a patriarchal society in tension with the women's conduct. In 1 Timothy and Titus the ideal of the submissive woman appears but in a context that mixes the domestic with the community; that is, the author links the conduct of the household with the conduct in the household church and society.[32] This is why the domestic codes here are not so clear as in Ephesians and Colossians. The author of 1 Timothy and Titus has as his point of departure the conduct of the household according to the codes and is interested that this conduct be extended to the household church. It is not an accident that the author uses "household" (*oikos*) to refer to the church (*ekklēsia*):

> I am writing these instructions to you so that, if I am delayed, you may know how one ought to behave in the household of God, which is the church of the living God, the pillar and bulwark of the truth. (1 Tim. 3:14-15)

We find, then, not only an a-critical reproduction of the domestic codes but a conscious assimilation of these with the intention of putting the rich women in their place, according to the patriarchal ideal—but as women, not as wealthy. As to rich women, it seems as if the author is ambiguous about the values of society, defining the rich, among them the women, as generous givers, but who should not boast and claim honors (6:17-19); besides that, he reminds them that the love of money is the root of all evil. So we find a contradiction in the author: in a certain sense he follows the tradition of Jesus (6:3) with respect to the wealthy, but not with respect to women or slaves. The dominant patriarchal ideology is present here, as among the male thinkers and leaders of the time. Thus, when confronted with the struggles for power, the author totally delegitimizes the rich women—as women according to the patriarchal ideal; as rich according to the tradition of Jesus. From the perspective of gender and class the author wants to annul the participation of these dominant women. Since they are women, he wants them to be silent, not to teach, but to be submissive. Since they are rich, he wants their donations to be generous, but not to impose themselves because of their wealth and power.

If it is true that this situation occurs because of the power struggles in the household church, it should not seem strange that the author includes instructions directed to the slaves. That men and women slaves must be respectful to their masters and mistresses and serve them well is not a contradiction with the author's negative posture toward the rich and the love of money. The slaves can serve their masters and mistresses well because it does not affect the polemic of leadership with respect to gender. The concern of the author is not the same in relation to slaves: it was the surrounding society that disapproved of the mixing of distinct social strata within the same community. We will look into this further on. We will now go deeper into the author's theological reasoning for his order of submission and obedience for women.

THE SALVATION OF WOMEN
THROUGH CHILDBEARING

The Text: 1 Timothy 2:13–3:1a

> [13] For Adam was formed first, then Eve; [14] and Adam was not deceived, but the woman was deceived and became a transgressor. [15] Yet she will be saved through childbearing, provided they continue in faith and love and holiness with modesty. [3:1] The saying is sure.[33]

Each one of the three verses shows a different aspect of patriarchal ideology: in v. 13 the order between genders; in v. 14 the vulnerability of women and the negative consequences of the lack of their own authority; and in v. 15, the salvation of women contingent on taking the role of motherhood.

To subordinate women, the author goes back to a common and well-known reading of the second chapter of Genesis conditioned by the patriarchal hierarchical ideology: Adam was formed first and afterward Eve. It is interesting that the text of 1 Timothy does not say that Eve was formed from the man. Here the verb *plassein* ("to form," "to mold") is used for both of them, but the author is interested in the order of creation. The sentence gives the understanding that God formed both. If that is so, it can be read not only in the positive sense—that women came from the hand of God, not from Adam's rib—but also in the negative sense, that this order was also established by God and therefore must be accepted.

If order is so important, it is because succession will have a certain relevance. It seems that for the author's mentality to be first means to be the firstborn, having certain privileges, as was usual in the Jewish and Greco-Roman cultures. In addition, to be first implied being better. It must be recognized that the conservative reading of v. 13 goes beyond the text and affirms that the second order implies subjugation. However, here the text at no time speaks of subjugation. It could even be said that the word "obedience" (learn with all "obedience") could be used in v. 11. In Greek *hypotagē* means "subordination," not "subjugation to man." Subordination in this case would mean to recognize that there is an order to which they must be subject. The order is found in the cosmos, the state, institutions, and the household. This order has a hierarchy, and in the case of gender the male goes first and the female goes afterward. In order to avoid chaos, the ancients thought this order must be respected.

Of course the distance between order and domination is very short, and that this order is conditioned by the values of the Greco-Roman society makes it very easy to read "domination and subjugation" or "superiority and inferiority" instead of "first and second." For this reason conservative readers see here an argument of Scripture to defend the submission of the women to their husbands and to men in general.

In v. 14 the author turns to Genesis 3, to the story called "the fall." By mentioning that account, the author wants to add that not only was Eve created in second place, but unlike Adam, she was deceived by the serpent. The author repeats the word *apataō* ("to deceive") twice, once referring to Adam (*apataō*) and the other time to Eve (*exapataō*). In the case of Eve, he adds the prefix *ex-*, which emphasizes the term even more: she was deceived "profoundly," "tricked" or "totally mocked." This verb could also have the connotation of "being seduced," which immediately brings to mind a sexual implication when applied to the feminine gender, again a representation of patriarchal ideology, because women are always associated with sex. In antiquity some Jewish thinkers, such as Philo, also saw in the Genesis text an allusion to the sexual seduction of Eve by the serpent. Therefore, patriarchal ideology still today assigns to women the well-known description of sinner, an easy prey to deception, given their erotic and nonrational character. Eve, says the text, after being totally mocked, became a transgressor or remained in the state of transgression; that is, she disobeyed God's commandment not to eat the fruit that had been prohibited to both of them, Adam and Eve. The first readers of 1 Timothy knew that account, which is why the author does not include the part about the fruit. Nor does he include that Adam also disobeyed upon eating the fruit and fell into a state of transgression. His readers also knew this. If the author does not specify here, it is because he wants to underline that the woman was the principal transgressor, being tricked by the serpent. For the author, the readers will understand that if Adam shared the transgression with Eve, it is because he obeyed her and accepted the fruit that she offered him. With this reading of Genesis 3, the author indirectly points to the negative consequences when women are permitted to teach and exercise authority over men (2:12).

The domestic codes of Greco-Roman society influenced the letter's reading of Genesis. The two accounts, that of creation and that of the "fall," redacted a thousand years earlier (tenth century B.C.E.) during the time of King Solomon, offered other contextual meanings that had nothing to do with the dominion of men over women, and vice versa. Besides that, some of today's rereadings, especially those by women, delegitimate oppressive readings of Genesis.[34]

Behind the author's theological interpretation of 2:13-14 is the analysis that young Timothy should make so as to carry out the author's mandate, namely, that all the women of the community, not only the two or three rich dominate women, should remember that their condition as women does not permit them to teach. The men of the community should not have to listen to them. Their condition does not permit it because they, by being women, are easily tricked and seduced by strange teachings (as was Eve, the mother of all the living), and they might teach that which is unadvisable. If they teach in front of the community, the men who listen could fall into transgression, as Adam fell upon listening to Eve.[35] To avoid "this catastrophe," according to the author, the communities should respect order: the women must become subordinate and stop dominating the men of the community. The author tells them that the women have their place ordained by God and must not usurp the place of men.

To quash the domination of rich women, who very possibly angered some of the male leaders of the community, the author uses the domestic codes, with the purpose of forbidding women to dominate men and to teach them (2:12). Women, according to the author, must assume their roles as mothers and occupy themselves with the managing of the household (2:15; 5:14). By speaking in generic terms, without speaking directly to the dominant rich women, the author responds to a very particular problem in a way that includes all women, independent of their class. The same thing happens with the story in Genesis that speaks of Adam and Eve as archetypes of masculine and feminine humanity (1 Tim. 2:13-14, see Gen. 2-3). In 2:15 the instruction extends to all women, beginning with Eve, passing through the Christian women in Ephesus and encompassing all women in all the world and at all times.

In 2:15 we find various textual difficulties. Literally, the text says this: "But she will be saved [singular] through childbearing, provided they continue [plural] in faith, love and holiness with modesty." The principal problem is theological, and the second has to do with the construction of the sentence, because the verb in the second part is plural but the subject is singular. The two questions that we need to respond to in order to understand the text are these: What does it mean "to be saved through childbearing," and who should continue in faith, love, and holiness?

But the most important question for this rereading is this: What would all this mean in the context of the Christian community of Ephesus and later in our context today?

The theological problem immediately appears if "salvation" is understood in the classical theological sense and not in the sense of "to be saved". This is because in the biblical tradition, especially the Pauline tradition, we are saved by grace, not by works of the law or by our own merits. Eve (or women in general)[36] to be saved has to have children. In this case she is saved by her own merits, and women who do not have children are not saved from the wrath and judgment of God. This would be a very strange understanding of the Christian tradition. But, to be frank, it fits perfectly within the context. Some scholars, to resolve this extraordinary position of the author, show that it deals with a physical, not a theological, question; namely, woman is saved from dying during childbirth, thinking of the "curse" of suffering pain during childbirth. It also can be interpreted in the sense that she, the woman, is protected from her deception upon taking the role of mother; that is, she is liberated from the devil and temptation. This interpretation also fits in the context of the polemics over gender roles.

Others see in the term "childbearing" (*teknogonias*) the Messiah,[37] the promised savior, who is the seed of life produced by Eve, mother of all the living, to whom it was promised that her descendants would strike the serpent on its head (Gen. 3:15). To see in the descendants of the woman (1 Tim. 2:15a) the Messiah would be a solution of salvation in the situation of her transgression, through which "sin" entered according to 1 Timothy 2:14. Curiously, in Romans 5, Paul sees Christ as the second Adam and the prototypical savior of the transgressions by the first Adam. Eve is not mentioned there as the transgressor.

It is true that it sounds strange to us that the verb "to save" (*sōzō*), connected here with "maternity," is used in a strictly theological sense. It would only make sense from the point of view of orthodox theology if "childbearing" refers to an understanding of Eve in relation to the promise of a future descendant (the Messiah), who would rescue her together with Adam. However, the author could very well have used the phrase (she will be saved through childbearing) from a spiritual or theological perspective to give paramount support to the command that women consecrate themselves to the household. In fact, his concept of salvation in other passages of the letter is somewhat unorthodox, as we will see in the third chapter. We remember also that in those early years of the church, there was not an orthodox theology, nor was the canon yet formed.[38] Rather, there were many currents of thought and various interpretations of Genesis. Besides that, we know that in some writings of the second century and beyond, alms were given a redemptive power.[39] That also seems strange to us. The purpose was to stimulate the rich to be generous in their donations to the church so as to help the poor. Someone wrote in the Second Letter of Clement (16:4) that alms were good, even as a penance for sins, and added that fasting was better than prayer, but giving alms was even better than prayer and fasting. He ends that verse with "Blessed is he that has been found with these virtues, because alms are converted into relief for the poor." Therefore, it is one thing to read the text and another to apply the text today. "To be saved" could be used in the soteriological sense in the exhortative and rhetorical discourse of the author, to convince the women of his community that they must carry out the roles that tradition has established for each gender. This would be the most difficult reading, given our beliefs today, but it is the one that best fits the problem in the Christian community at that time.

The problem of the plural in 2:15b, "they continue [persevere]" (*meinōsin*), leads us to ask, who are the subjects? The text says: "She will be saved . . . provided they continue." Who are they who persevere? The answers are diverse. It could be thought that it deals with the children of the woman; namely, that besides the requirement to have children to be saved, the children should be well brought up to persevere in faith and love and holiness with modesty. This interpretation gives the understanding that women's salvation is conditioned on the behavior of their children, which in traditional Christianity is also strange. Another very particular interpretation consists in seeing all of v. 15 as a continuation of the creation story including Adam and Eve in the plural: they, both of them, would be saved through their descendants; they are the ones who must continue in faith and love and holiness with modesty.[40] Nevertheless, the majority of interpretations propose that the subject is women in general; that is, from the first woman (Eve) the text skips over to the (Christian) women of history. In this case it has to be read that all women, like Eve, "will be saved" through childbearing and if they persevere with simplicity, modesty, and temperance (*sōphrosynēs*), in faith, love, and holiness.

In short, the proposals that come out of a text like this are various and sometimes contradictory. The most relevant is that the author chose the term "childbearing," which would imply for women that part of their role of managing the household (*oikodespotein* [see 5:14]) is the obligation to raise and educate children. Obviously, the author's intention is to take away the position that some rich and dominant women had assumed. In order to do that he uses the domestic codes in relation to the position and role that the patriarchal culture had assigned to women and propounds a theology with a concept of salvation very different from the Pauline tradition and the movement of Jesus. The author, like the thinkers of that time—we insist—wants to impose on women the role of the patriarchal household.

To have children (*teknogonias*) would also imply being married and forming a household. This is one of the important points of the argument in the letter. For this reason the text about the salvation of women by childbearing cannot be read independently of other texts such as 1 Timothy 4:1-3, where other teachings are strongly attacked and where it says explicitly: "They forbid marriage . . . ." For the author, those who prohibit marriage (and other things) "will renounce the faith by paying attention to deceitful spirits and the teaching of demons . . ." (4:1). Nor can the text be read independently of the dilemma of the young widows who have made the vow of chastity. The author states: "For I would have younger widows marry, bear children, and manage their households, so as to give the adversary no occasion to revile us" (5:14). We have, then, a problem that goes beyond the conflict with wealthy women benefactors. It is a struggle between genders apart from economic position. Although the starting point of the conflict is two or three rich women, it is possible that some men of the community (rich and poor) thought that the behavior of some women in the Christian community (rich and poor) was not appropriate because it did not conform to the domestic codes. Patriarchal ideology extends through all social strata, as we can state today in Latin America.

We will concentrate now on the case of the widows, one of the most intriguing or enigmatic passages in the letter.

THE OPTION FOR POOR BUT OBEDIENT WIDOWS

The Text: 1 Timothy 5:3-16

The theme of widows is something that attracts a lot of attention by those who study the First Letter of Timothy. The author dedicates fourteen verses (5:3-16) to the matter, which shows that it was a delicate situation that he believed had to be dealt with. The texts are very revealing, not only because they illuminate much about the roles of women but also for the richness and variety of details to be considered.

> [3] Honor widows who are really widows. [4] If a widow has children or grandchildren, they should first learn their religious duty to their own family and make some repayment to their parents; for this is pleasing in God's sight. [5] The real widow, left alone, has set her hope on God and continues in supplications and prayers night and day; [6] but the widow who lives for pleasure is dead even while she lives. [7] Give these commands as well, so that they may be above reproach. [8] And whoever does not provide for relatives, and especially for family members, has denied the faith and is worse than an unbeliever.
>
> [9] Let a widow be put on the list if she is not less than sixty years old and has been married only once; [10] she must be well attested for her good works, as one who has brought up children, shown hospitality, washed the saints' feet, healed the afflicted, and devoted herself to doing good in every way. [11] But refuse to put younger widows on the list; for when their sensual desires alienate them from Christ, they want to marry, [12] and so they incur condemnation for having violated their first pledge. [13] Besides that, they learn to be idle, gadding about from house to house; and they are not merely idle, but also gossips and busybod-

ies, saying what they should not say. [14] So I would have younger widows marry, bear children, and manage their households, so as to give the adversary no occasion to revile us. [15] For some have already turned away to follow Satan. [16] If any believing woman has relatives who are really widows, let her assist them; let the church not be burdened, so that it can assist those who are real widows.

The text is complex, because it presents various situations at the same time. It is necessary to read between the lines and to try to reconstruct the scenes to understand what it is saying. The first impression perceives problems of a diverse nature in which the economic situation of the widows, their comportment, their age, and their role in the church are all mixed together. There are poor widows who need economic help, widows whose conduct is reprehensible to the author, young widows who are "idle and busybodies," families who do not sustain their family widows, Christians who have widows in their household, and something very important—a special list of widows within the Christian communities. This list should distinguish between the widows of the community according to their age, economic situation, and conduct according to the traditional role of a widow in that time. The problems are more easily distinguished if we perceive the concentric structure of the text. We will read first without passion, and afterward interpret with passion and imagination.

A   Honor widows who are really widows (5:3).
    B   If a widow has children or grandchildren, they
        should make some repayment to their parents . . .
        (5:4-8).
        C   The list of widows should inscribe only those
            who do not have the following characteristics
            . . . (5:9-10).
        C'   Young widows should be excluded because . . .
            (5:11-15).
    B'   If a believer has widows, let her assist them and
        not burden the church (5:16a).
A'   So that the church can assist the real widows (5:16b).

It is very evident that there is an economic problem. It is immediately obvious upon looking at the structure's skeleton, above all in A B and B' A'. Let us look at A and A', which refer to the economic help that the church traditionally gives to the widows. The Greek word that has been translated as "assist" is *tima* (imperative of *timaō*), which literally means "to honor," "to respect." Besides meaning "to respect," this term can imply a payment of a donation or other material aid. The same term is used in 5:17, applied to the double payment or remuneration to the elders,[41] with the meaning of support, economic support. By using "really" (*ontōs*), the author wants, from the beginning, to restrict the help only to the most poor. We can verify this with B and B', which reflect more clearly the community's financial problem. Apparently, the resources were not sufficient for all the widows. Therefore, the author wanted to limit the help for the widows to those who were considered really widows, that is to say, totally defenseless. Who could take care of the rest of the widows? The author believes that if the widow has family members, they should support her (B). Or, if a wealthy woman already assists certain widows in her household (B'), she should totally support them so as not to burden the church, for the church can only take care of the poorest widows.

Nevertheless, the economic aspect can deceive us if we do not give proper attention to the dynamics of economic exclusion of B and B' and the qualifications of age and behavior to enter the official list of widows in C and C'. Moreover, the major problem concerns the admission to the list of widows of the church, not only because this matter appears at the center of the grammatical structure, but also because more verses are given to the young widows so as to exclude them from the list. We can now see that the problem of the widows goes beyond economic concern. The problem here in C and C' is not economic but rejection of the conduct of various women, particularly the young widows who did not adjust to the roles assigned by the patriarchal ideal that the author wants to impose. The same problem can be seen in part of B and B'. Now let us look at extrabiblical information to imagine what was possibly occurring with the widows of the Christian community of Ephesus.

It seems that in the community to which the instructions of

the letter are directed, there are many widows. One of the tasks of the first Christian communities was to take responsibility for widows, because in antiquity, with its patriarchal culture, a widow was a person practically abandoned and without rights because she had no man who could represent her.

Widows in Antiquity

In Jewish culture as well as Greek[42] most women depended legally and economically on men, first the father and later the husband and, in his absence, the oldest son. Women were represented by men, and it was supposed that men should stand up for women. Even wealthy widows who had power, status, and riches had to have a man to represent their interests. That person was called *kyrios* in Greek, which means "lord"; it could be her father, her husband—if she had one, a son, or another family member whom she would choose. In practice a wealthy woman, because of her power, could manipulate her *kyrios*.[43] The fact that women had legally to count on a man shows the patriarchal ideology. In those times the father of a woman, upon negotiating her marriage, had to pay the husband a dowry. If the husband died, she could stay in the household of her husband and depend on another *kyrios*, or she could return to her father; in that case the dowry would be returned to her father. The widow could marry again or look for a *kyrios* to represent her interests. In any case, widows could not represent themselves, and the reality was that there were many poor and abandoned widows because there was no one to defend them. In spite of the existence of rich widows with the power of the elite or the newly rich, in the scale of social stratification in the Roman empire, scholars of antiquity place widows in the lowest level. They were considered superfluous or expendable, even lower than slaves, together with prostitutes or textile dyers.[44] The truly wealthy widows were very few; the majority of widows were found in the lowest level of the population.

Within the Mosaic and prophetic tradition, widows, together with orphans, formed a group preferred by God because of their lack of defense in confronting institutions, poverty, and abandonment. The laws of the Pentateuch and the prophets defend them

(Isa. 1:17; Jer. 49:11; Zech. 7:10) as well as the Gospels (Matt. 23:14; Mark 12:40; Luke 20:47). The Letter of James states that religion that is pure and undefiled is to care for the orphans and widows and to keep oneself unstained by the world (Jas. 1:27).

The first Christian communities continued the tradition of the defense of widows among the very poor. In the Book of Acts we observe that community's enormous work among the poor, including the conflicts it raised (Acts 6:1). So for the recipients of 1 Timothy, the mention of widows and financial help is something familiar.

An Order of Widows

Now then, in the text we discover certain problems in relation to economics, as well as other problems that transcend the merely economical. On the one hand, the resources of the community are not enough, which means that there was a considerable number of widows. On the other hand, there is the other problem with a possible "order of widows" that had certain responsibilities to fulfill in the church. We know, from later letters of the church fathers that this order existed in the second and third centuries,[45] but we do not know exactly when it began. Today biblical scholars debate if it already existed when 1 Timothy was written. Some say no, since the text is not very explicit; but others say yes and argue that, because it was known by the recipients, there was no need to be specific. The text for some reason intends to limit the number and role of this order of widows. We believe, together with Bonnie Bowman Thurston, that, yes, there existed such an order and it performed important functions within the community, because in these first years within the Christian communities the women had the same roles in the church as men.[46] There were female elders and deacons, and also an order of widows.[47] This is not strange, because in Jesus' movement there were female disciples, and in the time of Paul there were female apostles of the same stature as Paul himself (Rom. 16:7). When 1 Timothy was written, there did not exist what we today call "bishops," named as the heads of the churches of a region. It is not known what exactly the specific tasks of the wid-

ows were. It is believed that the practices consisted of praying for
the community and making pastoral visits to the households. It
is quite probable that they also taught in the community and
took on other ministries. The restrictions that were made on the
women, in this and other letters and documents, suggest that
they had an active role.

Rules for Donations for Widows and for the Order of Widows

The letter tries to regulate both the donations and the order of
widows. Both cases would involve an economic factor, because
the order of widows could count on some honorarium, although
not necessarily. But the reasons are not only economic; they principally reflect patriarchal ideology, although both interests (economic and patriarchal) are mixed to such a degree that it is
difficult to separate them. In spite of the fact that these verses
seem to refer mainly to widows—to widows' families (5:4-8), to
young widows (vv. 11-15), and to the qualities of the widows in
the order (vv. 9-10)—the struggles for power by the male leaders and certain rich women could be present. The difference that
is established between the widows in vv. 5 and 6 is a social differences. The true widows are poor and totally abandoned. They
put all their confidence and hope in God. According to the
author, those who are not real widows are those who lead a comfortable life, living for pleasure (*spatalōsa*). In the Letter of James
(5:5), the author uses the same word for the rich landowners
when it says: "You have lived on the earth in luxury and in pleasure (*espatalēsate*)." According to the author of 1 Timothy, wealth
and a libertine life go together, although in practice this is not
always so. What is happening here is that the author wants to
remove those rich leaders who occupy posts simply because of
their power and influence, without being officially named. The
author tries to remove them by appealing to moral questions. For
us in Latin America, this is not difficult to understand, because
in many churches when those in authority wish to remove some
woman or even a man, they generally appeal to moral conduct.
In antiquity, the rhetorical discourse also used this argument.

Reading between the lines of the text, we see that it is probable that the author wants to take away economic support and erase from the list of the widows' order all widows, poor or not, who according to him do not fulfill the traditional tasks of the patriarchal household and prefer to be working in the church and for the Christian community. The author is worried that the community might be despised by the patriarchal Roman empire, but this text also reflects the conflict between these women and some male leaders about their functions in the community as men who have households and patriarchal privileges. This can be clearly seen in the case of the young widows and the emphasis that the author puts on the qualities that the widows must have to be in the list of the widows' order (5:9-15). The option for the poor widows in 1 Timothy depends on their obedience to the domestic codes.

The reasons for excluding church support for the widows who have possibilities of being cared for are logical: they can appeal to their families (5:4-8) or to a benefactor. The author does not want economic support for the widows who are staying in the household of a woman believer with economic resources who could well support them as a help to the community (5:16).[48]

There could be rich widows who did not need help or honoraria (if there were such) because they belonged to the order of widows. In this case, the church would not need to help them economically. The denunciation directed at the families that had widows and did not support them is so radical that it may refer to some rich woman who had a widow (mother, grandmother, mother-in-law, a husband's grandmother) in the family and was not taking charge of her but left her in the hands of the church.

The author launches his fury against wealthy women using his patriarchal arsenal against all women. He is not only against rich women but against all women, rich and poor, because they do not comply with the domestic roles. The young widows were not necessarily wealthy. They could be widows who were cared for by the church and therefore did not need to work in their parents' household in domestic tasks such as spinning and weaving. In the church these widows had time to visit the households and teach and console the families. As Irene Foulkes points out,

The greetings in Romans 16, with its praise of certain women for having "worked hard among you," makes clear their ample activity in the mission and teaching. Maybe this is what the patriarchal ideology of 1 Timothy would call "being idle" and "gadding about from house to house."[49]

The author exhorts them to marry and form a traditional patriarchal household and to keep busy in the tasks of the household and taking care of their children.[50]

The language that is used to refer to the young widows reflects a rhetorical discourse that does not have a real foundation but is part of the patriarchal ideology, with its gratuitous affirmations in the definition of women. Although it could be the case that some of the women in the women's order would want to marry again, the context of the whole letter points to the common myths against women. It is saturated with patriarchal ideology: "when their sensual desires alienate them" or "they are assaulted by pleasures and want to marry," "they are idle," "gadding about from house to house," "gossips and busybodies," "saying what they should not say" (5:13).

Today, in our patriarchal society, it is also still believed that a young widow "is crazy to get married again, has all the time in the world to gad about outside her home visiting neighbors, men and women, her head filled with nonsense, sticking her nose in everyone's business and talking all the time about nothing." A widow who does not stay in her house is called a "merry widow." But we know that her reality is other. The great majority of women-led households, widows or not, never have time for themselves, because they must work day and night to support their children. There are women in a more comfortable position, who therefore have time for other things outside the household. This does not mean that they are idle or gossips. In all societies there are huge challenges that women have to take on in order to become human beings. That there are women who gossip and are busybodies is evident; but the same is true of men.

Through the rhetorical discourse of 1 Timothy we can see that there were young widows who possibly belonged to a widow's order and did their work of pastoral visits. It seems that they had taken a vow of chastity (5:12),[51] as do today's religious orders. If the author wanted to restrict the visits of these women, it could have been for two reasons: because he feared that the order of the household would be subverted, or because what was being discussed in the household would be related to other teachings, since thanks to chastity the women had more freedom to be outside of the patriarchal household.[52] For this reason he wanted to restrict the order of widows by placing an age limit. At that time widows older than sixty years were very old women, without much energy to make visits and not a great danger. That is, they would not easily subvert the values of the household. Moreover, they probably would not enter into the power struggles within the house church. With the demands of a moral testimony, and with the requirement that they had been good mothers and wives faithful to the domestic code, the economic and ideological problems of the order were solved: fewer widows to support, more submission of the women, and fewer problems with the patriarchal imperial Roman society.

What the author wants to demand is that the church's single women abide by the domestic codes; that is why he gives the instruction that they "marry," "bear children," and "manage their own households" (5:14).

Though the author is clearly pro-patriarchal, among the reasons for his position we also encounter the fragility of the Christian community in confrontation with the government of the Roman empire, which saw danger whenever patriarchal household values were subverted. It is possible that in 5:14 the author refers to Greco-Roman society and not to those who are preaching another teaching—those who "do not recommend matrimony."

It could also be that the author is thinking that to carry out the mission of the church it is necessary to conform to the patriarchal values of the society that surrounds them; or he is considering the fact that the other teachings were becoming more evident through some women in the community of Ephesus.[53]

There are various reasons for the writing against women, but none of them can be completely justified. Obedience to the domestic codes that keep women in their households and excluded them from leadership and from their self-realization as human beings in other areas outside the home never can be a basis for the proclamation of the gospel and the reign of God, which speak of equality and justice. That would be an insurmountable contradiction.

We, the women of today's Latin America, are astonished at the similarity of the patriarchal ideology of that time to that of the twenty-first century. In the midst of today's scientific and technological development, the ideology of society and the patriarchal household continues almost the same, even in the developed societies of the West, in spite of the advance of many women. The assassinations, beatings, and abuse of women of all classes and social sectors, simply because of their gender, are evidence of the strong presence of this ideology. It is very painful to the Christian world that ahistorical readings of 1 Timothy and other texts, reinforced by contemporary patriarchal ideology, continue to legitimate violence and the depreciation of women.

Let us go on now to analyze the burning problem of different theological positions in the midst of these struggles for power.

3

Theological Positions and
the Struggles for Power

After reading 1 Timothy, we are drawn to see how certain communities produced a radical turn in the extraordinary Jesus movement and its early ambassadors that had started some seventy or eighty years earlier. This diversion was not general, because other communities at the turn of the first century conserved the initial practice of equality and solidarity with the excluded ones, as we can see from the Gospel of John or the Revelation of John or even the Letter of James. Yet frequently the experience of many women and men in today's churches is that their institutions reflect the instructions of 1 Timothy more than they reflect other New Testament communities that are more inclusive and democratic. Verticalism, the condemnation of those who do not think the same, submission to patrons, and imitation of dominant cultural values seem to reflect a literalist reading of this letter, which was written at another time for another community with its own problems.

All of this leads us to affirm that the letter should not be taken as normative, nor should it be rejected. Rather it should be considered as a very important document that permits us to see how the Christian communities were forming and institutionalizing the profoundly human conditions of their ecclesiastical and theological constructions. This is an inspired canonical writing, but one conditioned by its time. We also have to learn how to read this kind of letter.

In this chapter we will study the struggles between groups in the Christian community of 1 Timothy that had different theologies and lifestyles. A careful analysis of the letter in the context of the Ephesian community leads us to see that the author iden-

tified himself with one group and condemned the other. It also
permits us to notice the complexity of the problem, showing that
it is not possible to point to some as "the good ones" or others
as "the bad ones." Reconstructing the situation allows us to see
that the "bad ones" of the discourse are not so bad and the
"good ones" not so good and that these discussions are not very
helpful for the poor.

We have divided this chapter into five sections. The first tries
to reconstruct the situation in relation to what the author calls
"other teachings." At the same time we will see the problems
that are generated by the struggles for power being lived out in
the community. Here we will try to describe the groups and their
positions.

In the second section we will analyze how the patriarchal
Roman empire conditioned the author's solution and his preoccupation with mission and evangelization. We will dedicate the
third section to clarifying the author's theology and his strategy
in the theological discourse. In the fourth, we will study the
question of which of these positions favors the poor and
excluded, and the last section will be a general reflection on the
limits of tolerance, underlining the situations of intolerance or
the useless divergences in the letter.

THE DIVERSITY OF THEOLOGICAL POSITIONS
IN THE MIDST OF POWER STRUGGLES

We have seen in the earlier chapters that in the Christian community of 1 Timothy there were various conflicts. Moreover,
these conflicts deepened with the distinct theological positions
present in the community. From the tone of the letter, so
alarmed by the "other teaching," it seems as if these teachings
were well accepted by some of the members.[1] They even
opposed, according to the author, that which he considered to
be the Pauline and apostolic inheritance. These teachings were
a grave problem for him, which is why he refers to them at the
beginning, in the middle, and at the end of the letter. Let us look
at the beginning:

> I urge you, as I did when I was on the way to Macedonia,
> to remain in Ephesus so that you may instruct certain peo-

ple not to teach any different doctrine (*heterodidaskalein*) [that is, other doctrines or teachings]. (1:3)

In the middle we find the following:

Now the Spirit expressly says that in later times some will renounce the faith by paying attention to deceitful spirits and the teachings of demons. (4:1)

And at the end there are two texts:

Whoever teaches otherwise and does not agree with the sound words of our Lord Jesus Christ . . . . (6:3)

Timothy, guard what has been entrusted to you. Avoid the profane chatter and contradictions of what is falsely called knowledge (*gnōseōs*). (6:20)

If we distance ourselves from the author's excluding affirmations and look closely at the text, trying to reconstruct the situation, we observe that there were divergent views among the members of the congregation. It is not about a heretical thought from outside of the Christian community that was being introduced into the church. The teachings to which the author refers already enjoyed acceptance and were possibly gaining ground among the members.[2] For the author, these teachings were detrimental not only at the level of ideas but principally because of their influence on the members' conduct. The author had a moral position that corresponded to the Greco-Roman social and cultural vision that surrounded him. This position clashed with the theoretical position and conduct of the others, which made them his adversaries in this letter.

We know that at that time there was no canon or unified teaching.[3] A first canon was formed in the year 200, that is, one hundred years after the writing of this letter. So the theological position of the author was one among others. It was not "the" theological position of a pure apostolic or Pauline tradition. Such a thing did not exist; there were various positions. In fact, it can be shown that the "others" who taught "something different" also claimed to belong to the Pauline tradition, as occurred years later. This can be clearly observed in the apocryphal writing *Acts of Paul and Thecla* (see Appendix II below), which presents some similar characteristics of "those who teach otherwise" and claim to be followers of Paul.[4] Thus, we find two distinct teachings that clash. Both, as shown by Lewis R. Donelson, are products of creative theology, belonging to the historical moment in which they were born.[5] Both have negative and positive elements.

Unfortunately, we cannot know directly the group condemned in the letter; we have only the description of them. Besides that, the author is not interested in describing their teaching; he is interested only in discrediting them. So the references to "whoever teaches otherwise" are very general and difficult to identify with a certain group or tradition. Scholars debate whether the letter deals with the characteristics of the pre-Gnostics or belongs to Hellenistic Judaism, or both of them. We believe that both elements are present.

It is important to understand that the bellicose and condemnatory manner in which the author attacks those who think in another way belongs to the rhetorical style common in antiquity. As the majority of the commentaries indicate, the author uses the same stereotypical argumentation that the Greek and Latin philosophers used against philosophic positions different from their own. For them, the others are usually greedy, libertine, charlatans, hypocrites, vicious, and so on. The purpose of the rhetorical style was to persuade and convince the readers or audience that the others were wrong. One of the ways of doing that consisted of polarizing the positions and, in this way, strongly condemning the others, to the extreme of demonizing them. Our author does that in 1 Timothy 4:1-2. As can be seen, with this literary style there is no possibility of knowing the "other" or of an invitation to dialogue.

There are two specific elements that the author condemns—directly or indirectly—and they are apparent in spite of the rhetorical style. These elements are a sophisticated reasoning that leads to endless arguments and certain ascetic attitudes toward marriage and some foods.

Let us start with the direct manner of confrontation in the text. In the first place, the author criticizes abstract and sophisticated reasoning that generates much debate and discussion (1:3-4; 4:7;

6:3-5; 6:20). He advises his delegate Timothy not to pay attention to "myths and endless genealogies" (1:3-4). The text could
allude to Gnostic elements that have to do with aeons (emana-
tions of a supreme being) and interpretations of creation outside
of the Jewish tradition.[6] But it could also be said to allude to a
current of Hellenistic Judaism with Gnostic tendencies that prac-
ticed this kind of abstract or enigmatic reflection on ancestors.

It could be that the author thought that the "others" felt
superior to the common people, because they devoted themselves to abstract arguments and emphasized knowledge. It was
not in vain that they called their movement "science," which the
author said was "falsely called science" (*pseudōnymou gnōseōs*
[6:20]). 1 Timothy 6:4 criticizes this sense of superiority by saying that these others are puffed up (*tetyphōtai*), or that they are
conceited or filled with pride but in reality understand nothing
but to argue and dispute, which only leads to envy, dissension,
slander, and the like (6:3-5). In 1:7 he says that they believe
themselves to be "teachers of the law" but do not even understand what they say.[7]

The author repeats several times his negative attitude toward
this verbiage and speculation, because for him these others detour
from what is central, which is to carry out an administration (plan)
of the household of God (*oikonomian theou*) "that is known by
faith" (1:4b) and not to get lost in sophisticated arguments. What
is essential, he adds, is "love that comes from a pure heart, a good
conscience, and sincere faith" (1:5). Further on we will analyze the
translation and the significance of *oikonomian theou*.

It is for this reason that the author insists that Timothy keep
himself apart from these persons, not fall into the trap of their
arguments, and be a model in his word and conduct; that he
practice justice, godliness, and other good things; that he give
attention to the public reading of Scripture, exhortation, and
teaching (4:6-16; 6:11-12). Timothy should, above all, affirm
and guard "what has been entrusted" (*tēn parathēkēn* [6:20]) to
him. The author does not specify "what has been entrusted," but
it probably refers to the tradition left by Paul. This term and
"sound teaching" (*hygianousa didaskalia* [1:10]) are used only
in the Pastoral Letters and show the importance of claiming the
Pauline and apostolic inheritance.[8]

The expression "what has been entrusted" or "the deposit" was a legal term to refer to a place where money, properties, or some valuable knowledge was kept.[9] For the author, the entrusted tradition was very highly valued, and "the others" were turning away from it with their sophisticated arguments. According to the philosophers of antiquity "the sound teaching" meant that which was reasonable and sensible. Sound teaching, idea, opinion, or thought was for the Greeks "the correct," "the reasonable."[10] It is interesting to note that Paul never used this term; for him the gospel of Jesus Christ was not sensible or reasonable but "foolishness" (1 Cor. 1:18). Of course, Paul did not agree with sophisticated arguments that understood nothing, because his communities, although they included some benefactors, were composed of "common" people of modest resources (see 1 Cor. 1:26-27).

The author of 1 Timothy does not define "the deposit," "sound teaching," or "the sound words of Jesus Christ." As we said above, he is interested not in theoretical debate but in condemning the teaching of others. The meaning of "the deposit," "sound teaching," and "the sound words of Jesus Christ" must be deduced from the contents of the whole letter. That includes not only the theological affirmations but also the exhortations. So then, for example, it is probable that "the others," because of their dualism, reject the humanity of Jesus: "For there is one God; there is also one mediator between God and humankind, Jesus Christ, himself human" (2:5). For the author, this affirmation is "the knowledge of the truth" (2:4b). We find the same in 3:16 when, in his definition of the "mystery of our religion," he writes: "He was revealed in flesh," that is, bodily.

The sophisticated position of "the others" suggests a privileged educated group with time to discuss and speculate. We know that the Gnostics were a small and select group. According to them, salvation was reserved for those who arrived at the full knowledge of God through their science. Perhaps because of this, the author indirectly speaks of a soteriological universalism,[11] among other things. That is, all, not a select group, have access to salvation (2:4) "because we have our hope set on the living God, who is the Savior of all people, especially of those who believe" (4:10).

The second explicit characteristic of those who did not think as the author is the ascetic attitude concerning marriage and certain foods. In 4:3a we read: "They forbid marriage and demand abstinence from foods. . . ." In this same text the author responds directly against abstention from certain foods when he says: ". . . which God created to be received with thanksgiving by those who believe and know the truth" (4:3b). The two following verses in this chapter theologically reject the abstinence from certain foods, pointing to the creation of the world and matter as something good.[12] The author writes: "For everything created by God is good, and nothing is to be rejected, provided it is received with thanksgiving; for it is sanctified by God's work and by prayer" (4:4-5). It could be that the others reject wine, as did certain groups in antiquity. The author mentions wine three times: he advises Timothy not to drink only water but to drink wine for the sake of his stomach (5:23); and he exhorts the candidates for elders and deacons not to take too much wine (3:3, 8). In spite of all we have seen up to now, it does not seem that the greatest problem for the author was asceticism in itself but the influence this could have on peoples' conduct, especially the rejection of marriage.

Abstention from sexual relations was not foreign to certain religious currents of the time. Taking into account the somewhat authoritarian character of the author, asceticism would not have been a problem for him (authoritarianism and asceticism often go together), if it were not for the concrete situation in which his community lived in relation to two aspects: the struggles for power, especially with the wealthy women, and the imperial, patriarchal Roman society, as we will see further on.

The author shows very clearly his position in favor of marriage, declaring that the salvation of women is through childbearing and care of the family (2:15), as we saw in chapter 2. In the Ephesian Christian community we observed that possibly the widows who entered the church's list made a vow of chastity. The author wants to impede the young widows from adopting this custom; in fact, he wants them to marry. His reason is that they might break their vow to Christ: "when their sensual desires alienate them from Christ, they want to marry, and so they incur condemnation for having violated their first pledge" (5:11-12). The author expressly wants Timothy to change this practice of the young widows. He exhorts them to marry, have children, manage their households well, and not give a pretext for the enemy to speak badly of the Christian community. The criticisms here cannot come from those who "teach other doctrine," because those are just the ones who are against marriage. The criticisms probably come from the Roman imperial society. The situation, as we can see, is very complex; it mixes the power struggles with the wealthy women, the relationship of power between the genders, and the threatening context of the Roman empire.

It has been thought that the theological position of "the others" was caused by the emancipation of groups such as women and slaves, by the relativization that diminished the importance of history through the concentration on knowledge and the privilege of reason. The Second Letter to Timothy adds the belief that the resurrection has already happened (2 Tim. 2:18); it is probable that "the others" mentioned in 1 Timothy shared this position, which would cause them to diminish the importance of history. According to some commentators, this attitude automatically led to scorn for the authority of the state and the patriarchal family, as well as the official leaders of the church. We know that Gnostic groups in the second century shared this vision.[13]

Confronted with the position of "the others," the author responds with a contrary position. With respect to the prohibition of marriage and the leadership position of the women (possibly single, rich, and looking for power in the community), the author turns to the traditional domestic codes of the patriarchal Greco-Roman culture. With this he intends to check both fronts: the ascetic position and women who are teaching in the community. According to the domestic codes of the household, women should listen in silence and should not exercise any authority over men. They should dedicate themselves to childbearing and care of the family (2:11-15). The slaves, for their part, should honor their masters, believers or not (6:1-2). The fact that within the Christian community they called themselves brothers and sisters should not give space to equality between slaves and masters. Speaking of state authority, the author does not relativize it but asks that the people pray for kings and authorities so that they may live in peace and tranquility (2:1-2).

We can see the same thing with respect to church authorities.

If previously the deacons were the supervisors (*episkopoi*), now it seems, according to the text, that they looked to impose one supervisor (*episkopos*), possibly a coordinator of the deacons, who would have greater authority. On the other hand, if the community accepted the author's instructions about the characteristics of the supervisors (3:1-7), there would be no space for more inclusive elections, including, for example, slaves or poor persons who were "not respectable" according to Greco-Roman society, or women, because they were prohibited from teaching. We will look at this point in the next chapter.

In sum, we find in the community a group that was proposing a different theology from that of the author, with reference to theological abstractions and ascetic attitudes (rejection of marriage and abstention from certain foods [4:3]). It seems as if this thinking of "the others" was well accepted by various members, especially by the women, because indirectly it affirmed their emancipation from the patriarchal household by prohibiting marriage and permitting them to take on leadership roles, independently of the official rules or authorities.[14] In the struggles for power within the community, the discourse of "the others" gave a certain advantage to these women.

Now then, inasmuch as this manner of thinking was sophisticated, only a privileged, educated group with time to discuss could embrace it, which leads us to think that these are wealthy women, benefactors who are most likely to be receptive and to promote it. Because of this, and the struggles for power, we can understand the authoritarian tone of the author against the women. The author believes it necessary to combat the theological thinking of "the others" and to declare it damaging and demonic (4:1-2), something that does not correspond to the "deposit" of the apostolic and Pauline tradition, which was sound and correct. But the struggles for power do not explain everything. The imperial Greco-Roman society conditions the intolerant argument of the author.

THE CONDITIONING OF THE IMPERIAL ROMAN SOCIETY

The conflict generated by those who thought in another manner was not only a question of content; it was not just that it taught asceticism and sophistication. The fundamental problem was, as we said earlier, the behavior provoked by the theology of "the others" in a specific context. We have already mentioned the struggles for power within the community. Now we will consider the influence of the imperial Roman society.

Like all the authors of the New Testament writings, our author is interested in evangelization and mission.[15] At the end of the first century and the beginning of the second, in the midst of so many theological currents, he is interested in affirming a certain Pauline identity as "the true tradition."

Various passages show the interest in mission for the salvation of the world (1 Tim. 1:15; 2:1-7). For the author, this could be hindered if the internal tensions continued and if the conduct of certain members of the community was not in accord with the patriarchal culture of imperial Roman society. The context of the empire conditioned the conservative vision of the letter, because the sphere in which mission and evangelization were to be carried out was hostile.

At that time, the imperial society considered Jews and Christians suspicious because of their monotheism, which was incomprehensible in a polytheistic world. In fact, in different parts of the empire there were persecutions against them because of their refusal to worship Caesar. The Romans were very jealous of their customs. The criticisms that some ancient writers leveled against Jews could also be made against the Christians. Of the Jews it was gratuitously affirmed that they separated themselves from other people and tried to distinguish themselves within the towns. They proselytized, sent money to Jerusalem, and were the enemies of all human beings; they hated God, were anti-Roman, and were against the family.[16]

To be against the family or the organization of the household was a political insult in the Roman context, especially within the aristocratic sphere. The second-century apocryphal work *Acts of Paul and Thecla*, even though it is fiction, is a very clear example of the mode of thinking at that time. In this work (see Appendix II) the heroine Thecla refuses to form a family so that she can instead follow Paul, which was the reason that the authorities burned her alive. Even her own mother felt dishonored by her daughter's decision. Let us look at this text:

The governor of Iconium asks Thecla:

"Why will you not marry Thamyris, according to the law of the Iconians?" But she stood looking earnestly upon Paul, and when she answered not, her mother Theocleia cried out, saying: "Burn the lawless one, burn her that is no bride [celibate] in the midst of the theatre, that all the women which have been taught by this man may be affrighted."

Before Paul and Thecla were brought before the tribunals, Thamyris, Thecla's betrothed, questioned two men who were hotly arguing about Paul's message. He interrupts and asks them: "You men, tell me who you are, and who is he that is inside with you, who makes the soul of young men and maidens to err, deceiving them that there may be no marriages but they should live as they are." The two men, Demas and Hermogenes, respond: "Who this man is, we know not; but he defrauds the young men of wives and the maidens of husbands, saying: 'You have no resurrection otherwise, except you continue chaste, and defile not the flesh but keep it pure.'"

The story of Thecla reflects the gravity of the decision to not form a family, especially among the aristocracy. For the Romans, the collapse of the family meant the collapse of the state. At that time, Roman women and those of other cultures were being emancipated from the patriarchal household, as we saw in the last chapter. The Roman masculine aristocracy did not look favorably upon women who became emancipated; the Greek and Latin philosophers, as well as the historians and the satirists, also criticized the free behavior of the women, especially the matrons.

We could say that the Jesus movement, which spoke of equality and considered women and slaves to be autonomous subjects, was absurd for a patriarchal and slave state. The conduct of this egalitarian community was an aberration in a highly stratified and patriarchal setting such as the Roman society.

Now then, at the time when 1 Timothy was written, Christians' presence was more visible and awkward. Because the author was worried about the safety of the community and also about opportunities for mission, he opted to follow the values of the patriarchal household, which he very probably also shared. Thus, he wanted to apply to the church these same imperial patriarchal domestic codes (3:4–5:12). This can be seen in three instructions: according to the author's criteria, the supervisor must be well thought of by the outsiders (3:7); slaves must consider their masters worthy of all respect, so that the name of God not be blasphemed by those who do not belong to the community (6:1); and finally, the young widows should marry, have children, and manage their households well so as not to give the enemy a pretext for speaking against them (5:14). All these texts show the author's preoccupation with the Roman society. He was concerned that the Christian community not be seen as a conspiracy group against the empire that was contrary to its interests and culture.

The position of "the others" against marriage could be politically dangerous if in the Ephesian community the women followed that "other teaching." In this sense, it is not foolish to affirm, as does Jouette Bassler, that for many restless women of that century, to leave the patriarchal household was an emancipation, and for that reason the "other teaching" could have been well received by them. One of the issues within the Christian communities may have been that the freshness of the Jesus movement and its inclusion of women were being set aside at that time.[17]

The conduct of the women, according to the author of 1 Timothy, could be counterproductive in the cultural context in which they were living; it could generate more hostility and at the same time be an obstacle to the evangelizing mission. Maybe that is why the author combats "the others" and asks his delegate Timothy to declare "the good fight of the faith" to "save the sound doctrine." The thinking of "the others" must not put the community or its mission in danger.

THE THEOLOGICAL RESPONSE OF THE LETTER TO THE INTERNAL AND EXTERNAL CONFLICTS

Having situated the theological positions of the groups in conflict—and the imperial Roman context—we will now look more thoroughly at the theology that the author elaborates to respond to the internal and external conflicts of the Christian community.[18]

At first sight it seems that the author does not elaborate a coherent theology but repeats theological declarations and liturgical fragments already known. For example, one does not see in the author of 1 Timothy the same systematic theological and influential creativity that Paul showed in Romans or in Galatians. Various scholars have been critical of this author's apparent lack of cohesion. Recently, however, commentators who understand the limits of the letter have seen in his theology a coherent proposal narrowly linked with his ethic.[19] For us, it is also very clear that the theology and the conduct that he demands are articulated in a very conscious manner. We can see in his theology his own strategy, elaborated in such a way that he develops a concrete and effective discourse that has the intention of resolving the conflicts and winning the battle, sacralizing his position.

If we keep in mind all the elements implied in the conflicts, we can see that the author is not an authoritarian person who without any motive seeks to impose the values of the patriarchal Roman society, just because he wants to. Neither does he invent a theology that has nothing to do with his reality. For him the Christian community of Ephesus needs an intervention that has credibility and will help to resolve the conflicts. Therefore, he proposes to respond effectively, for which he elaborates a theology of salvation intimately related to his exhortations, instructions, and counsel. The thesis of Yann Redalié is exactly this; for Redalié soteriology and parenesis are the motor of the whole discourse of the Pastoral Letters, which is constructed to deal with two questions: the time that passes and has to be confronted, and the social space that has to be occupied.[20]

The author of 1 Timothy intends, with his theological proposal, to solve all the problems—internal and external—in which the community is involved: the intellectual theological fight; the wealthy, especially women patrons who want to dominate, ignoring the precepts that ruled the Christian community; and the imperial Roman society that threatens the existence of the Christian communities.

Let us look at our author's understanding of salvation and

observe how his theology is ambiguous. On the one hand, he distances himself from imperial religion, which sees the emperor as savior. On the other hand, he assumes the values of Roman society for the survival of the community.

God and Jesus Christ Are the Saviors

Already at the beginning we find important data. The first thing that gets our attention is that God appears as Savior (1:1), because in the other New Testament writings, excluding Timothy and Titus, it is Jesus who carries this title. We know that this is nothing new, because in the Old Testament Yahweh is Savior and Lord. But the author of 1 Timothy assigns God the title of Savior, not to follow the Jewish tradition but to oppose the Roman emperor.[21] At that time emperor worship was common, and Ephesus was one of its most important locations. The emperor was called Savior (*sōtēr*) and Lord (*kyrios*), and in 1 Timothy God is Savior and Christ is Lord (1:1-2). The emperor was considered to be the *paterfamilias,* and the God of the Christians is called Father (1:2). The emperor was considered to be an apparition of God; the emperor's presence was spoken of as an epiphany (manifestation). 1 Timothy also speaks of the manifestation (epiphany) of Jesus Christ (6:14). For the author, Christ Jesus is the true mediator between God and human beings (2:5).

There is, then, a deliberate application to God and Christ Jesus of the Hellenistic terminology that described the emperor. Some commentators think that the terminology was used to acculturate Christian theology by using the same religious language, adapting it to the context in which the church was evolving. We believe, however, as does Philip Towner, that, by using the titles commonly given to the emperor, what the author is doing is contrasting the Christian religion with the worship of Caesar.

The author was interested in two things in relation to the concept of salvation: first, to make clear that the true Savior and Lord was not the emperor, but God (2:3), through Jesus Christ, God's mediator; second, that all human beings could be saved, especially the believers (4:10). We could say that the universality of this salvation did not have as its first intention to make Christianity the only true religion and to condemn all the rest, but rather to reject the worship of the emperor and the belief that the emperor was the manifestation (*epiphaneia*) of God. The author introduces in the first and last chapters two doxologies that proclaim the greatness and uniqueness of God. In 1:17 he writes: "To the King of the ages, immortal, invisible, the only God, be honor and glory forever and ever. Amen." In 6:15-16 we read: ". . . he who is the blessed and only Sovereign, the King of kings and Lord of lords. It is he alone who has immortality and dwells in unapproachable light, whom no one has ever seen or can see; to him be honor and eternal dominion. Amen." This conclusion could be rejected if one read 2:1-2 as if the author were in agreement with the politics of the empire and had opted to accommodate to its values to live peaceably. At least many have understood the following text in that way:

> First of all, then, I urge that supplications, prayers, inter-cessions, and thanksgiving be made for everyone, for kings and all who are in high positions, so that we may lead a peaceable life and in all godliness and dignity. (2:1-2)

We interpret it in a different manner. For the author it was important that the Christian community survive and continue growing in the hostile context in which it lived.

The author uses four different words when he asks his members to pray so that they may live peacefully: "supplications," "prayers," "intercessions," and "thanksgiving." The reiteration shows that the people's endurance was not easy in the surrounding atmosphere, and they had to strengthen themselves through prayer. The intercessions are for everyone; nevertheless the emphasis is placed on the kings and all the state authorities, which could mean that the hostilities first came from them. To live quietly (*ēremon*) and peacefully (*hēsychion*) suggests living without threats, without pressure from the tribunals, to live in peace. Paraphrasing the text, the author is asking that the community intercede before God for all human beings, especially for the authorities, so that they will leave them in peace and that then his members may continue living with dignity and exercise their religion without being disturbed.

In a situation like this, the message of salvation of the only saving God and God's only mediator, Jesus Christ, could be preached more clearly in contrast to the official emperor worship. But while the prayers were becoming reality, the author had to continue preaching and "keeping the commandment (*entolen*) . . . until the manifestation of our Lord Jesus Christ." To be a follower of Jesus could run risks, including appearances before the tribunals, as Jesus had to appear before proconsul Pilate and "made the good confession" (6:13-14).

It is probable that these theological declarations could also have been affirmed by the other group of the community who "taught different teachings," in the sense that their enthusiastic position (in which the resurrection had already happened[22]) and metaphysics led to the relativization of authority. However, the author distanced himself radically from their ascetic position, as we have seen, above all with respect to marriage and food. The author declares explicitly that this God, Savior of all human beings (2:4; 4:10), immortal, unapproachable, and invisible, is also the Creator God who gives life to all things (6:13-16).

According to the author's theology, everything created by God is good, and therefore all food should be eaten; nothing should be rejected "if it is received with thanksgiving." Food is doubly blessed: by God's word, which says that creation is good, and by the prayer of the believer (4:3b-4). The same applies to the couple, although this specific section does not refer explicitly to women and men as creation intended for reproduction. It would have to be understood in that way, because the letter is in favor of marriage.

On the other hand, the author's Christology emphasizes the importance of history and the flesh, namely, matter. The author has in mind the ascetic group, not only the emperor, when he affirms that Christ Jesus is the mediator between God and humans, repeating it so that it would be clear that this Christ Jesus is also human (*anthrōpos* [2:5]). In 3:16 he reiterates the same when he speaks of the mystery of our religion: "He was revealed in the flesh," meaning in a body.

Now, let us look at the author's interpretation of salvation on the basis of obedience to the institution and the ethical mediation required.

Godliness as a Condition for Salvation

To identify God as Savior was not the most important thing for the author. All his readers already knew that God was the Savior, the same as Jesus. What was important for the author was a concept of salvation that would respond to the internal and external conflicts of the community, that is, what he would say about how God's saving action was made effective through the redemptive act of Christ Jesus.

The author articulates salvation in terms of the conduct of everyday life. It is not that he affirms that salvation is by works and not by grace. According to the testimony of the author, who calls himself Paul, it is clear that one is saved by grace. In 1:15 he repeats the confessional phrase, "Christ Jesus came into the world to save sinners," and he affirms that Christ saved him. In this same text he affirms that the grace of the Lord overflowed in him (1:14). Again in 2:6 he takes up the confessional phrase: "Christ Jesus . . . who gave himself a ransom for all." It is evident, however, in various parts of his discourse that certain conduct and religiosity (godliness) are a fundamental condition to receive the salvation given by God, or an unconditional expression to refer to this given salvation.

Salvation is seen as a process in which two epiphanies of Jesus Christ intervene; here is his great creativity.[23] An appearance or manifestation (*epiphaneia*) occurs at the beginning, at the moment in which Jesus lives on the earth, and the other at the end of time, when Jesus comes at the final judgment. Between these two appearances the participation of the believers in salvation takes place, and the real effectiveness of salvation given by God depends on the way they live in this space and time.

For the author, the will of God is that all be saved: "God desires everyone to be saved and to come to the knowledge of the truth" (2:4). He explains this truth in the following verses: "For there is one God; there is also one mediator between God and humankind, Christ Jesus, himself human, who gave himself a ransom for all" (2:5-6a).

For the author, with Jesus salvation was being inaugurated in human history. This "truth" was the testimony of God's universal saving will, which arrived in an opportune time (*kairos*

[2:6b]). In this text, the historical appearance (*epiphaneia*) of Jesus Christ is alluded to, although not using the word *epiphaneia* for the historical life of Jesus as in 2 Timothy and Titus. But he alludes to it when he refers to God's incarnation in history to save humankind.

The author uses Paul's biography as evidence of this salvation. Christ, who came to save sinners, saved Paul so that he would serve as an example for future believers so that they could also inherit eternal life (1:16). After that, it will depend on the believers to receive salvation or not. The author then tries to teach the members of the Ephesian community the concrete way to achieve salvation. It is here that we find difficulty with the theology and with the practice, because through his teachings and above all his exhortations, the author articulates salvation with a style of life similar to the ideal conduct of imperial Greco-Roman society, where the patriarchal household is central. This theological strategy is very clear in 2:15, where he affirms that women will be saved if they have children, meaning if they fulfill the role of mothers and provided that they or their children continue in faith, love, and holiness with modesty.

We have seen that the term "godliness," or "holiness" (*eusebeia*), is a key to the letter. It not only connotes faith in the "mystery of holiness" (3:16); it also includes the idea of taking on a religious life reflected in appropriate conduct. In this sense the required qualities of the community leaders as well as Timothy himself would enter the realm of godliness. For the author, godliness, as well as the body, needs to be strengthened, and that is possible only through persistent dedication. This is why he writes: "for, while physical training is of some value, godliness is valuable in every way, holding promise for both the present life and the life to come" (4:8).

According to the text it is precisely the "training" of godliness that will save now and in the future. That is why, for the author, "the others" who had another teaching were lost with their intellectual exercises, which were pure fables. At different points in the letter the exhortation to godliness appears. To Timothy, the virtual recipient of the letter, the author exhorts: "Have nothing to do with profane myths and old wives' tales. Train yourself in godliness" (4:7). "Profane myths," "old wives' tales" is the contemptuous way in which the author evaluates the theology of those who propose novel elaborations in line with myths, genealogies, or stories like Thecla's.[24]

In 4:16 the author again underlines that salvation is received depending on one's practice. He clearly says to Timothy that, if he follows exactly the instructions given, including the public reading of the Scriptures, exhortation, teaching, not neglecting his charisma, staying away from those who profess "other teachings," being a model, and so on, he will be saved with those who follow him: "Pay close attention to yourself and to your teaching; persevere in these things, for in doing this you will save both yourself and your hearers" (4:16).

Finally, eternal life, which would mean salvation obtained in its plentitude at the end of time, was something that Timothy should grasp. He had been called to it, had confessed it before witnesses, but had to take hold of it (*epilabou*), conquer it, and not let it escape (6:12-14). This, for the author, would be obtained only by fleeing from those who did not think as he did, so he could "run behind, pursue" justice, godliness, faith, love, endurance and a humble heart" (6:11).

In 6:18-19 the author returns to relate salvation (in this case "eternal life") to good works. The rich will be saved if they practice goodness, do good works, give generously, and do not set their hopes on riches. With these actions they will acquire true life.

Now then, negative conduct that was not in accord with what the author thought was correct living also worked against their salvation. Hymenaeus and Alexander "suffered shipwreck in the faith" and because of that were expelled from the community (1:20). Also some young widows, who left their role as wives and mothers by not marrying, "turned away to follow Satan" (5:15). The same thing happened to those who were tempted by the love of money: "some have wandered away from the faith and pierced themselves with many pains" (6:10).

Perseverance in godliness, understood as we have seen, must be maintained until the second appearance (*epiphaneia*) of Jesus Christ—sent by God at the right time—that is, until the second *kairos* (*kairos idiois* [see 6:14-15]).

Before going on to the next point, let us ask ourselves: How does the author respond to the internal and external conflicts with this theology of salvation and godliness? The answer—indirectly of course—is not difficult. With respect to the dangers of the hostile imperial society, he proposes that his Christian community, who are participating in a process of salvation, have a conduct that would not represent any danger of rebellion against authorities, nor against the slave owners. Their training in godliness includes conduct in accord with the highest virtues of Roman society: seriousness, moderation, humbleness, and observance of the domestic codes with respect to wives, children, and slaves. Even more, with that kind of behavior, it was possible to convince those outside that the Christian religion (piety, godliness) would go beyond imperial worship, whose piety (*eusebeia*) was limited to perfectly controlling the rites[25] independent of people's lives. Thus, instead of seeing in the Christian liturgical meetings a conspiracy against the empire, the neighbors should see a model to follow and therefore also obtain salvation. The will of God, for the author, is that all be saved, not just Christians, although especially them (4:10). The life of Christians was itself a message. Besides offering "sound teaching," Christians should invite others to imitate them, so that they might be saved by God through the only mediator between God and humankind, Jesus Christ (and not the Roman Emperor).

With regard to the conflict with the rich members of the community, especially with the rich women, the author responds explicitly: the rich, men and women, should help the church economically and be generous, if they want to have true life. By fulfilling that role in the community they will achieve salvation. Women—all of them, but especially the wealthy ones involved in the struggles for power—instead of teaching and looking for leadership roles, should rather dedicate themselves to good works and the household, have children and bring them up in faith, love, and holiness. Only in this way will they be saved (2:9-15).

Those who "were teaching different doctrine," for the author, were totally lost; there will be no hope for them if they continue thinking as they do and behaving as they behave. Because salvation is not obtained through ideas and pedantry without end, but by leading a godly life until the second *kairos*, in which Jesus Christ will appear again to judge.

The Church and Its Leaders as the Guarantee of the Knowledge of the Truth for Salvation

Because the basic problem is the struggles for power, the author cannot put aside the institution of an order that must be obeyed. In fact, the whole letter is like an exhortation to obey the legitimate authorities of the household, the church, and society. For the author, in that context, the members' conduct has to be controlled; therefore he makes clear who should be the legitimate authority that teaches sound doctrine and the true godly life that leads to the salvation that God desires.

Both texts, 1:3-4 and 3:14-15, are important because they are related to (1) the presence and the absence of the author in the community; (2) the sending of the delegate Timothy to the Christian community of Ephesus; and (3) the letter's proposal. In 1:3-4 we read:

> I urge you, as I did when I was on my way to Macedonia, to remain in Ephesus so that you may instruct certain people not to teach any different doctrine (*heterodidaskalein*), and not to occupy themselves with myths and endless genealogies that promote speculations rather than divine training (*oikonomian theou*) that is known by faith.

The theological disagreements within the community were the straw that broke the camel's back in the conflicts. The author felt that it was urgent to do something, so he left his delegate Timothy in Ephesus so that he could begin to confront the situation: to stop those who were teaching different doctrines and at the same time give support to the elders "who teach and preach well" (5:17). For the author these disagreements generated more conflict and disorder in the household of God.

The key words in 1:4 are *oikonomian theou*.[26] The term has to do with administration, direction, or planning of a household or a government; in this case it would be the church. The type of theological debate held by those who were teaching different doctrine, according to the author, promoted disputes and did not allow good church direction or administration according to God's will. Administration must be grounded in faith, faithful to

God and not to ethereal reasonings. So the author was interested in winning the battle by imposing order and limiting teaching; the theological discussions, according to him, accentuated the problem instead of helping to resolve it.

1 Timothy 3:14-15 is clearer with respect to the writer's proposal:

> I hope to come to you soon, but I am writing these instructions to you so that, if I am delayed, you may know how one ought to behave in the household of God (*oikos theou*), which is the church of the living God (*ekklēsia theou*), the pillar and bulwark of the truth.

The author left Timothy in Ephesus, but according to this text he hopes to be present also, although later. Because the situation seems to him to be urgent, however, he does not want to let more time pass and sends a letter before his arrival, in case he is delayed. With these details the author constantly marks his presence and his authority as a recognized apostle.

The text reveals his intentions. What is important for the author, as we have been saying and as is written here explicitly, is the conduct of the members of the Christian community. It is not accidental that these texts appear after the exhortations to the women and immediately after describing the qualities of all who aspire to be official leaders. Two elements are profoundly revealing. The first is the combination "household of God" and "church of God," as well as the term seen in the previous verses: "the administration of the household of God" (*oikonomia theou* [1:4]). This is the authority that is assigned to the church.

With regard to the first element, we observe that the author wants to make the church (*ekklēsia*) a household (*oikos*). This can be seen as positive in the sense that a household seems familiar, less formal, while the church seems like a very structured institution. At that time, however, the situation was the opposite. When the household (*oikos* in Greek) was spoken of, it clearly referred to a patriarchal institution. In chapter 2 we saw the characteristics of this household, which by definition is hierarchal and authoritarian. There is only one patron who has the power; the wife, children, and slaves are considered his property and they must obey unconditionally. The word "church" (*ekklēsia* in Greek) has the connotation of a democratic citizen's assembly of the Greek cities. All those meeting, without exception, could speak and had the power of decision making. Free men met in the assembly to deliberate democratically the matters of the city. The council, or *boulē*, gathered the accords, and the governor carried them out. Of course neither women nor slaves participated, because they were not citizens. The term *ekklēsia* also reflected the sense of the Hebrew word *qahal* ("assembly") as it appears in the Greek translation of the Hebrew Bible (the Septuagint).

The Christian ekklesia was a democratic assembly in which all persons could participate, independent of their social condition or gender.[27]

So the text astutely makes synonyms of the patriarchal household (*oikos*) of God and the church assembly (*ekklēsia*) of God. The domestic codes, which in 1 Timothy appear scattered (2:9-12; 3:3-4; 6:1-2) and without the reciprocity that appears in Ephesians (5:12–6:9) and in 1 Peter (3:1-7), are to be applied not only within the private household but in God's household, meaning God's church. This "ecclesiological strategy" could not be more clear in 3:4-5 in the description of the quality demanded of the supervisor:

> He must manage his own household well, keeping his children submissive and respectful in every way—for if someone does not know how to manage his own household (*oikos*), how can he take care of God's church (*ekklēsia*)?

What the author wants to say is that conduct within the church must be the same as the conduct of the patriarchal household. The church must have only one maximum authority, to which all the members must submit. Let us remember that the author no longer speaks of supervisors in the plural but a supervisor (*episkopos*). He would have the role of father, and all the other members would have the roles of sons and daughters, if not obedient servants. The women, wives or mothers, could neither teach nor be leaders, for as in the patriarchal household they must listen with total submission (2:11-12). Notice that if delegate Timothy were able to apply all these instructions, the democratic feature of the *ekklēsia* would disappear. With this step from *ekklēsia* to *oikos* (household), the author intended to unify, among the members of the community, behavior in the three social spaces: the patriarchal household, Roman society, and the Christian community. That is how he sought to resolve the conflict of the internal struggles for power and to soften the hostility of their imperial context. In this way "they could remain in the world."[28]

In addition, however, the end of 3:15 says clearly that the (patriarchal) household of God, as the maximum authority, was the true institution: "the pillar and bulwark of the truth." With this radical affirmation, it was assigning to the institution the power to determine which was the true theology, the "sound teaching," and which was demonic (4:1). The institutional church was the institution that had the "deposit" of truth.

As to the author himself, he chose the identity of the apostle Paul to give force to his words: by doing so, he was assuming an authority and a tradition that had a lot of weight for his hearers. This was important for the author, because as we have said, it is possible that those who thought in another manner also declared that they belonged to the Pauline tradition.

The biography of Paul, to which the author dedicates several verses (1:12-16), not only is a credible account but also serves to invite his readers to imitate him. In this account he includes Paul's conversion and his subsequent exemplary conduct; he proposes Paul as a paradigm of behavior.[29] It is noteworthy that Jesus, in spite of the declarations about his role as mediator and Savior, appears to be on a second plane, under the shadow of the apostle.

Timothy is exhorted to be an example to the believers; the author constantly reminds him (three times in this brief letter: 1:18; 4:14; 6:12) of his legitimacy as a leader for having been ordained by the elders. With that, he expressed that the legitimate authority was passed by means of ordination, not by status, favoritism, or even a calling by the Spirit. This was his concept of church, his ecclesiology, which had a specific proposal for a certain context two thousand years ago, namely, to resolve struggles for power and theological disputes. Let us go on now to make an evaluation of his position.

AN OPENING THAT EXCLUDES AND
AN OPTION FOR THE POOR
CONDITIONED ON OBEDIENCE

Let us consider now all the elements together and evaluate them. We will return to the positions of the two groups (one is "the others" and another supports the author) and ask ourselves which of these discourses favors the option for the poor and women. In which elements do we really find the tradition of the Jesus movement or its negation? Let us also examine what have been the consequences of these theologies and the literal application of the letter.

To untangle the skein of all these elements is not easy, but it is clear that one cannot opt for any of these positions. The most that can be done is to understand the situations that generated these discourses and choose constructive elements that edify and promote human dignity in general and the dignity of women and the poor in particular, that is, to act in accordance with the gospel of Jesus Christ.

We are confronted with two conflicting theological positions that influence the conduct of their followers. Proponents of each say that they are true and possibly heirs of the Pauline tradition. One is called "other teaching" by the author and is condemned by him. This teaching, however, had been well accepted by some members of the Christian community of Ephesus. The other is the position of the author, which he calls "sound doctrine" (1:10), "deposit" (6:20), and in agreement with "the administration of the household of God" (1:4).

With regard to these two positions, we are interested in analyzing two aspects: respect for human life, especially women and the poor, and respect for diversity of thinking that does not damage or exclude persons. Looking at what we have studied above, it seems to us that in both positions there is exclusion of the poor, both men and women. Even if there is an opening for them, their possibilities of full participation are closed.

Let us start with the position of "the others." We have to proceed carefully, because we know them only through those who condemn them and through hints in certain extrabiblical documents. We dare to say that within this group there is what we could call an "opening that excludes." This seems to be a paradox, but that is how we perceive its thinking in its totality. We say "opening" because it relativizes authority and order—in a social context where stratification and hierarchy were considered natural and were desired according to the dominant philosophies. This position opens the way for all persons, independent of their gender and class, to enter; however, in practice the opening was only for some. From the beginning this group, which tended to elaborate a sophisticated, argumentative theology that generated disagreements, ran the risk of excluding those who had neither intellectual preparation nor sufficient time for discussion. Here the excluded would be men and women of scarce resources. The characterizations "speculations" and "meaningless talk" come from the author of 1 Timothy, who is not impartial; nevertheless, the frequency of the critique is an indication that this was a real perception.

Further, a position that does not demand marriage might seem to be attractive to women who would prefer an emancipated life outside of the patriarchal household; Christian women would have the freedom of choosing a greater dedication to teaching and leadership within the community. However, this eventuality was surely restricted to wealthy women because of motives mentioned above. A better way of leaving the patriarchal household was the order of widows, because this would include poor women. Another alternative would be married women whose partners were looking for an alternative family, different from the patriarchal family and more in line with the principles of the Reign of God.

A "charismatic" group, who believed that the resurrection had already taken place,[30] and who relativized authority and earthly order, unfortunately also relativized with the same intensity human history, suffering, struggles, and aspirations. This group opted for knowledge and not for people of flesh and bone.

Our author, for his part, is right to criticize abstract and sophisticated arguments that oppose those with a simple message of love among human beings, a pure heart, a good conscience, and sincere faith (1:5). The problem is his patriarchal authoritarianism and his assimilation of the cultural values of imperial

Roman society, even though his intention was to safeguard the mission. We indirectly find a certain option for the poor when he criticizes the rich and those who want to be rich, as well as when he opts for the real widows, meaning those really abandoned (5:3). However, his basic option is questionable in the sense that he does not respect widows as subjects of their own history. His option for the poor is conditioned on their being obedient. Chapter 5 of the letter, which discusses the problem of "rebellious widows," allows us to make this affirmation. Neither can there be a real option for women when they are excluded from teaching. The option for poor widows fails upon promoting the option of living in the family's patriarchal household and in the patriarchal church. The patriarchal household reflects the values of a society of patrons and slaves, of a dominating family master and submissive members, of an emperor with subjects and vassal peoples.

The beginnings of the Jesus movement are clear about the special attention given to those who had been excluded, the poor and women. There were no conditions. Besides, according to the Gospel of Luke, God has revealed the mystery of God's Reign to the little ones (see Luke 10:21). We also know that in the beginning women were great leaders of the churches and were involved in all kinds of ministries. Therefore, what we see in 1 Timothy is not only that the author is against the dangerous consequences of emancipation in the theology of "the others," but that ultimately he is proposing to retreat from the egalitarian and democratic experience of the first Christian communities.

For today's readers, the principal problem has been the consequences of taking the author's discourse literally. In the second and third centuries, in the midst of tensions and tendencies, this letter was used frequently to silence all women—not only the wealthy—and to exclude them from leadership and significant participation in worship. Today this letter continues to be used by churches that reject the ordained leadership of women. Read literally, the letter has served to legitimate hierarchal positions and attitudes of intolerance within the church. The fundamentalism of our time has roots in this document, which explains why such fundamentalism is profoundly patriarchal.

BETWEEN INTOLERANCE AND
USELESS DIVERGENCES

To conclude this chapter we want to reflect in a general way about tolerance and intolerance and the useless divergences that we observe in the disagreements presented in the text. To reflect on these aspects is important today because we live in an atmosphere of war and hostility between civilizations and we feel the need for interreligious dialogue.

According to Ángel Ocampo, a Costa Rican philosopher, human history is full of conflicts that are the inevitable result of the diversity among human beings.[31] The way in which we confront such conflicts can lead us to the destruction of some by others, if there is no room for tolerance. But tolerance moves between two poles: absolute relativism, thanks to a tolerance without limits, and blind absolutism, thanks to an intransigent intolerance that also denies limits for intolerance. Because of this, what is most important for Ocampo is to approach tolerance starting with its limits, especially of its foundation. And its foundation is the living subject (person)—as an organic network of interrelated humans with their concrete needs—that establishes the criteria for the limits of tolerance and intolerance faced with the ever-present plea of "the other." So there is no way to disregard the limits or to absolutize them. The first leads to permissiveness and the acceptance of pain and death, and the second leads to the crushing of persons (subjects) when the limits of intolerance are suppressed. If one position leads to silence in the face of genocide, the other can lead to genocide. Finally, then, what measures tolerance or intolerance is not so much the content of the disputes as the consideration of the human being, the living person. With this contribution of Ocampo, let us now analyze the text.

One of the most important aspects of the hermeneutical process is to try to understand the reason for the writing of the letter. We have already spoken about the struggles for power and a group within the community that taught different doctrines that the author did not consider correct. We would have to suppose that those who thought and taught different doctrines also believed that their theology was correct. We have, then, two different theological points of view. Both are interpretations of an

inherited Pauline theology. In order to evaluate these interpretations, we begin with the living human being. For the group
who "thought differently," most important were ideas, "science," and knowledge; the real person was not important, even
though their position could indirectly generate the emancipation
of some social sectors. By scorning matter and human history,
they scorned the person, who for them was without sex or class.
Indirectly, their ascetic position toward marriage led in a certain
sense to emancipation for the excluded, because this theological vision diminished the importance of human history, the patriarchal household, a person's body, and the authorities. However,
the emancipation was not in function of the person (as subject,
agent, or actor). The negative vision of matter is already a negation of the person. Besides, the incitation to emancipation did
not necessarily mean that their vision of gender was egalitarian,
because the women leaders who were able to do so became masculinized, as we observe in some earlier Gnostic texts.[32]

The author's own position is clearer because only he speaks.
By his authoritarian and hierarchical tone we can affirm that his
position is one of intolerance when confronted with other ways
of thinking. It is clear that intolerance polarizes and demonizes,
so it is then that the author demonizes the other teachings (4:1)
and authoritatively sanctions them, excluding "the others," who
for him have deviated from the faith ("whom I have turned over
to Satan" [1:2]).

We have already seen that, among the reasons that led him to
adopt an intolerant position, was the survival of the Christian
community in a hostile context. We saw that his intolerance was
exacerbated by the dominant presence of the women benefactors
or patrons, who quite probably were those who supported the
other theology. If this corresponds to reality, his position might
seem valid at first glance because he is interested in the life of real
persons, and this is the most important hermeneutical criterion.
All tolerance should have a limit, and the criterion of the limit,
according to Ángel Ocampo, is the living person. However, the
position of intolerance is called into question when this proposal
to resolve the internal conflicts and to assure the survival of the
Christian community in the Roman context affects persons in a
negative manner, in both their relationships and their human

dignity. The author negatively affects women and slaves by using the domestic codes to resist any kind of emancipation of the patriarchal household in the repressive context of the patriarchal imperial society.

The attitude with which the domestic codes were imposed on the *ekklēsia* in the context of the Roman empire has been called "loving patriarchalism," with the intention of justifying the author's position and his concern for the survival of the Christian community. However, in 1 Timothy we do not see any attitude of love; rather we perceive an authoritarianism toward those who "think in another way" and toward all the members of the community. It is an authoritarianism that seeks to be legitimated by the Pauline tradition and by the gospel, itself converted into law. For Luise Schottroff, "loving patriarchalism" is very important for an ideology of domination. It means a "condescending love" on the part of those who are above "in exchange for obedience of those who are below."[33]

The author is concerned that his members have acceptable conduct in consonance with the values and virtues of Greco-Roman society, so that they will be approved and not be seen as dangerous. At the same time, however, he is concerned that the preaching of salvation and liberation in Jesus Christ be extended to all the nations so that they might be saved. Again we run into two problems: first, Christians would have to enter into dialogue with the religious experiences of other peoples and not impose their own religion; and, second, according to the author, the possibility of carrying the mission to the nations demands a respectable testimony in consonance with society's values. This last presents a problem in relation to the values themselves, for slaves and women are asked to be obedient to the patriarchal household in order to have success in the mission. From the point of view of women and slaves, that mission, the preaching of the good news, is a sign of an alienation from the values of the kingdom proclaimed by Jesus and his disciples. In other words, it manifests a break with the gospel's content itself, which proclaims equality for all human beings and God's preferential love for the excluded.

We find ourselves confronted with a dilemma: On the one hand, there was the danger of being eliminated by the forces of the empire. By affirming that "there is no longer Jew or Greek, there is no longer slave or free, there is no longer male and female; for all of you are one in Jesus Christ" (Gal.3:28), Christians professed values that contradicted those of the reigning society. On the other hand, assimilation of imperial values led to the submission of those excluded. Carried to the extreme, therefore, if we opt for emancipation, we run the risk of losing our life; if we opt for assimilation, we will have a servile future, far from the proclamation of the message of salvation—if this is not understood simply as salvation of the soul without the body.

The Gospels do not present this dilemma; they call only for following Jesus and his prophetic practice. But we need to understand that the early church, at the beginning of the second century, began institutionalizing itself and faced challenges when it realized that the second coming of the Reign of God was not imminent. The disagreement went beyond the debate of those who "teach different doctrines" of Gnostic tendencies—whether Hellenistic Jews or not. The churches of the second century were in a certain sense clandestine, because the worship of Caesar was obligatory, and their monotheistic religion did not allow them to participate. This was also a time in which the wealthy began to increase within the churches and theological creativity generated quarrels.

In this situation, the institution—order and law—was important, but not necessarily the institution as the author conceived of it, in the sense of a law that punishes, a law for the disobedient and for those who think in another manner (1:8-11). The institution should have the capacity to conduct the processes of dialogue and the ability to discern important elements of different theological creations: those that help in the dignification, liberation, and edification of persons, and especially theological thought that does not exclude women because of their gender and embraces the poor and those who suffer discrimination. Divergences are useless in moments of crisis and political repression: the wearing down of disagreements can divert the principal foundations of the kingdom proclaimed by Jesus in the Gospels. And the apostle Paul in Romans 14:1–15:17 exhorts mutual respect with regard to different food and different religious practices: "For the kingdom of God is not food and drink but righteousness and peace and joy in the Holy Spirit" (Rom. 14:17). The contribution of Paul in Romans concerning grace and law is extremely important, if grace and faith are interpreted as realities that infuse the law or the institution. A law or an institution under the horizon of grace gives preference to the real living person. It does not blindly impose nor absolutize but places itself at the service of the life of persons. Jesus splendidly expresses it in the Gospels: the Sabbath was created for the service of humankind and not humankind for the service of the law (Mark 2:27).

Institutional leaders should not stamp out theological creativity, because the risk of thinking in another way is good and can enrich the knowledge of God. Leaders should have the capacity to discern the times and to know the persons who would benefit by such teaching and also to evaluate the practice that these theologies generate. They should be watchful for useless and harmful divergences and know when theological proposals move away from the principles of the kingdom proclaimed by Jesus Christ, which are oriented toward the common good, justice, solidarity, peace, and love.

In our time respect for the other is an urgent call. Christianity, "imperialized" by Constantine in the fourth century, filtered the interpretations of Scripture based on interests far removed from those of Jesus Christ, the peasant of Galilee. The colonial readers of 1 Timothy easily found fertile ground to universalize circumstantial positions and make them sacrosanct. The leaders of the Christian communities in the second and third centuries who won the theological disputes and formulated a tradition to follow laid the foundation for a way of being church that even today seems impossible to demolish. Some Protestant churches have been able to democratize the institutional church with the participation of women in all leadership roles; however, it still remains to recreate an ecclesiology with more flexible structures, where power struggles are set aside and where all members, men and women, really feel included.

Although this reflection could sound like a final conclusion, it is not, because we cannot finish a book on the struggles for power in the early church without first analyzing the criteria for leadership positions in the Christian community of 1 Timothy. We will deal with this in the next and final chapter.

4

Criteria for Leadership
in the Struggles for Power

In this chapter we will deal with the positions of leadership in the community or communities meeting in houses. One of the problems we take on is that neither the titles nor the functions are very clear. We believe that 1 Timothy was written in a period in which the structure of the church was still not defined, and therefore we find a certain variation with regard to the titles for the different tasks of leadership. So, for example, the qualities of the supervisors (*episkopoi*) in 1 Timothy are prerequisites that Titus requires for the presbyters (*presbyteroi*).

LEADERSHIP POSITIONS
IN THE BEGINNINGS
OF THE CHRISTIAN COMMUNITIES

In 1 Timothy the following titles or positions are named: "supervisor" (*episkopos*) in the singular, in charge of "supervision" (*episkopē*), "deacons" (*diakonoi*), "presbyters," or "elders" (*presbyteroi*).[1] Also mentioned are particular prerequisites belonging to a special group composed of "widows" (*chērais*), which may mean that there was an order or a ministry for a group of widows, as we saw in chapter 2. This does not mean that at that time there existed three different and defined positions, plus the order of widows, as in the letters of Ignatius of Antioch. Here in our letter the structure of the church has to be deduced from the context, because the author does not explain it: The receiving community may have known perfectly well of what the author was speaking.

To begin, we must look very clearly at the word *episkopos*,

which some versions of 1 Timothy 3:2 translate as "bishop." It
does not correspond to what we today understand by "bishop,"
meaning an authority who is in charge of various churches and
to whom all the clergy and the communities should submit
themselves. This bishop, called a monarchic bishop by scholars,
does not correspond to the early times of the Christian communities. The English word "bishop" comes from the Latin *episco-
pus,* which in turn comes from the literal transcription of the
Greek *episkopos,* which simply means "supervisor," "overseer,"
"protector," "guardian," "vigilant." In fact, that is the oldest
function of the presbyters: to be vigilant supervisors. In those
early times of the first century, the Letter to the Philippians,
directed to one church, speaks of bishops in the plural (1:1). In
Acts 20:28, written before the *First Letter of Clement,* the *Pastor of Hermes,* and the letters of Ignatius of Antioch, when Paul
exhorts the elders of Ephesus (Acts 20:17), he says to them:
"Keep watch over yourselves and over all the flock, of which the
Holy Spirit has made you overseers (*episkopoi*), to Shepherd the
church of God. . . ." From the text of Acts, we see that the role
of the presbyters or elders was to be bishops in the literal sense
of the term, that is, caretakers or those responsible. In Acts 14:23
"elders" were appointed for the different communities that were
being founded. The text says: "they had appointed elders for
them in each church . . . ," meaning that they were appointed
to be responsible for the communities. Thus, if we find a coin-
cidence in the function of bishops and elders, as in Titus and very
possibly in 1 Timothy, it probably refers to the same persons and
not a mixing of traditions.[2]

The term "deacons" also appears in the plural (see Eph. 3:7;
Phil. 1:1; Rom. 16:1); in Greek it means "servant," "one who
serves," and as a leadership position "minister," "one who min-
isters." The deacons' functions were not those of mere assistants;
the term is very extensive, because besides serving the Christian
community, the deacons preached, evangelized, and taught, as
was the case with Stephen, Philip, and also Phoebe.

Before the institutionalization of the church, the structures of
the Christian communities were varied and flexible; all responsibility for leadership in the community was seen as a gift of the
Holy Spirit. There were no officials whose authority was given
through ecclesiastical means.[3] There was much space given to

prophecy, and persons with this charisma were seen as filled with the Holy Spirit and were given great respect and acceptance in the communities. Because leadership had to do with a gift of the Holy Spirit and not an institutional assignment, persons of any social class or gender could become leaders. Women had ample participation in the communities, thanks to this gift, and therefore participated in the leadership with authority. That is why it is very probable that there were not only female deacons but also presbyters and/or elders.[4]

In the first decades of the Christian era, before the writing of the First Letter to Timothy, it was never only one person directing the community or the communities; nor was there talk about only one presbyter as the supervisor (*episkopos*). On the contrary, it seems as if there was a college of presbyters, men and women in charge of watching over the church (*ekklēsia*) to help it to move forward. The fact that 1 Timothy uses the singular *episkopos* does not mean that in this letter the function of bishop was established as it came to be known later.

In 1 Timothy we still do not see the later rigid structures. It is true, though, that, because of distinct reasons that were expressed earlier, the letter intends strongly to restrict, through certain requirements, the participation of women, even in the ministry of the widows. Nevertheless, to speak of the qualities of supervisor or bishop in the singular does not refer categorically to their functions as such but to the qualities, above all moral qualities, that they should have in order to be assigned. The same is true of the qualities to become a deacon and to enter the widows' list (5:9-15). Curiously, and this is important, in the letter the qualities of the presbyters (elders) are not mentioned, and the reason is probably that they had already been described when referring to the supervisor (*episkopos* [3:1-7]) because they were probably the same.

What is new in 1 Timothy is the singular use of the term "supervisor" or "bishop" (*episkopos*), which at first glance gives the impression that in the time that the letter was written there was already a head that governed the Christian community, but we insist that that was not yet the case. The letter is prescriptive, not descriptive. However, by the singular use the letter is giving an initial step toward a patriarchal hierarchical structure. It is said that 1 Timothy reflects the transition[5] between the episcopate as a collective function of supervising and administering the community and the later "monarchic" episcopate, whose functions were no longer simple supervision and administration of economical and liturgical activities but governing all the communities. This occurred when the bishop, besides the economic administration, assumed the tasks of teaching, prophecy, and interpretation.

There are two possibilities for the singular use of *episkopos* in 1 Timothy. The first is that it could have been a singular collective, which means that there were various supervisors. The problem with this interpretation is that immediately after the letter refers to the deacons not in the singular but in the plural (3:1, *episkopos*; 3:8, *diakonoi*). The other possibility is that the letter deals with one presbyter among a group of presbyters named to be the supervisor.[6] We are inclined toward this second alternative. In 5:17-22 we find references to the preaching, teaching, salary, accusations, and ordinations of presbyters.

In sum, it is probable that in the Christian community of 1 Timothy there were three groups who had responsibility:

1. A kind of college of *presbyteroi* within which one person was elected as supervisor (*episkopos*) or coordinator of the group of men and women presbyters of the Christian community. Their mission was to facilitate order in the activities and administer the money. The *episkopos*, if in fact he was the head of the circle of presbyters, was also at their service and elected by them for a certain period of time. Authority was centered in the college and not in the supervisor. Because it is very probable that there were women presbyters, they could also be elected *episkopos*. It is possible the Eucharist was celebrated by a presbyter, woman or man, because at this time women still had not been excluded from these functions.

2. Male and female deacons. These persons, besides collaborating with the presbyters in all the activities, whether liturgical or service to the poor, made pastoral visits, taught, preached, and very probably baptized along with the presbyters. Surely many women exercised this ministry.

3. A ministry of widows with certain tasks such as prayer, pastoral visits, or teaching.

The author of 1 Timothy instructs his delegate, Timothy,

about the prerequisites for those who aspire to leadership positions. Although the author probably was not inventing a new order, he was conferring a special place on the *episkopos* as "guardian" of the traditions and as father of the church. All this was done with the intention of restricting the leadership of women in the Christian community because of the power struggles with the women and those who proposed "another teaching."

THE SUPERVISOR, THE COLLEGE OF PRESBYTERS, AND THE STRUGGLES FOR POWER

The text that precedes the list of requirements is curious. Instead of beginning directly with the necessary qualities for supervisor, the author begins with the common saying "Whoever aspires to the office of supervisor, desires a noble task."[7] Given the context of the struggles for power, we have to read this verse with shrewdness. In a normal situation one would begin directly with the list of requirements for the supervisor, deacons, and widows. But, as the situation of the community is conflictive, we see indications of real aspirations to the position of supervisor. It is possible that there were various persons who wanted to be leaders, and maybe they did not even form part of the college of presbyters. But who were these persons? If our suspicions are right, those who aspired to this position were wealthy persons, including those women who, by being patrons or benefactors, believed they could assume leadership without being candidates. We have read between the lines and have tried to reconstruct the situation. Two contexts have to be discerned: that which could exist independently of the letter and that which the letter tries to create. Both situations are problematic.

The first situation could be the following: In the community of 1 Timothy there were female as well as male leaders: female presbyters (elders), deacons, widow organizers, teachers, preachers, prophets—very active women, as in all the first Christian communities. These women would have come from different social strata. We know of the existence of female slaves who were prophets or deacons,[8] for example, as well as persons having some social position. If a woman benefactor wanted to impose herself, it would generate an abrasive, uncomfortable situation, especially within the group of men and women presbyters, in particular the men. Even when a woman belonged to the college of presbyters, there would be friction if she behaved like a supervisor. This was not because they were jealous or ambitious, but simply because they conducted themselves according to the customs of antiquity in the social and religious associations.[9] Within the Christian communities, heirs of the values of the Jesus movement, the situation would not be acceptable.

Here we must reread the texts about the presbyters. The author's proposal is that they should be paid double,[10] especially those who work hard in the teaching and preaching.

> Let the elders [or presbyters] who rule well be considered worthy of double honor, especially those who labor in preaching and teaching: for the scripture says. "You shall not muzzle an ox while it is treading out the grain." And "The laborer deserves to be paid." (1 Tim. 5:17-18)

According to these verses, the presbyters, and not only the supervisor (*episkopos*), governed or watched over (*proestotes*) the community. It must be assumed that some women formed part of the college of presbyters, because they had not yet been excluded from leadership. Men and women taught and preached. It is interesting that the author instructs Timothy to give double payment to the presbyters who worked hard (*kopiōntes*) in teaching and preaching, which were the most important areas. This is noteworthy, because, according to 5:4 and 5:16, there are economic problems in the community concerning, among other things, maintaining the poor widows. If the author asks that they be paid double, it is possibly because other important elements are present. According to our suspicions, it could be that the male and female presbyters were not well off and that the presence of rich men and women in the community, who also wanted to govern, teach, and preach, produced frictions with the official authorities. Because of the proposal to pay double, we can deduce that the social position of the men and women presbyters was not taken into account by the wealthy men and women, as it should have been, placing them in an embarrassing position. So then, the wealth and power of social status comes into conflict with leadership and official status—all within the cultural framework of honor and shame.

The force of the author's discourse against the women (2:11-12), analyzed in chapter 1, makes us think that the major conflict was being produced especially between the men leaders and the rich women. According to Elisabeth Schüssler Fiorenza, after bishops and deacons gained influence and assumed other functions of leadership, the influence of the wealthy members diminished and fell under the control of the administrative authorities of the church.[11] This is not yet the case in 1 Timothy, but it is that struggle for power that generated the discourse in which the authors sides with the ecclesiastical authorities. The problem is resolved several decades later in detriment to women, rich and poor. According to L. W. Countryman, the tension with the wealthy resolved itself when rich men were chosen for the position of bishop, as in the case of Polycarp, bishop of Smyrna.[12] But let us return to our text.

The following verses could also be an indication of the conflicts between these sectors:

> Never accept an accusation against an elder except on the evidence of two or three witnesses. As for those who persist in sin, rebuke them in the presence of all, so that the rest may also stand in fear. (5:19-20)

The fact that the letter mentions accusations against presbyters and attempts to regulate the process can, in this conflictive context, reveal that there were irregular accusations. These accusations without the proper procedures could have come from the small group of wealthy persons who believed they had the green light for any action in the community, just because they were benefactors, men or women. The imperative "never accept," or "never receive," is categorical and means to terminate the anomalies or injustices of the accusations. The public alert could occur within the circle of presbyters only or in the presence of the whole community. The text is not specific.

1 Timothy 5:21-22 again refers to the problem of the power struggles, the prejudices and favoritisms that could be found in

the community in relation to the naming of the presbyters. Let us observe the tone of the imperative:

> In the presence of God and of Christ Jesus and of the elect angels, I warn you to keep these instructions without prejudice, doing nothing on the basis of partiality. Do not ordain [lay hands on] anyone hastily, and do not participate in the sins of others; keep yourself pure.

The tone is very solemn; it could be that this was one of the crucial matters for the community. The aspiration to leadership (3:1b) was being converted into a struggle for power, and the young Timothy ran the risk of being on the side of the patrons because of their strong pressure on him. The author solicits Timothy, in the name of God and Christ Jesus and the angels, not to "lay hands on," not to "ordain," precipitously. In other words, the young Timothy must think very carefully before the laying on of hands for the naming of the leaders.[13] Possibly behind the text was strong pressure from those who had power and means in the community and who wanted to govern. Timothy needed to follow the established procedures to avoid prejudices (*proskrimatos*) or favoritism (*proklisin*) at the hour of the "laying on of hands."[14] It seems as though the author did not want the dominant rich women in the college of presbyters, but he does not say so openly. He says it indirectly when he details the qualities of the *episkopos*. The way was already prepared in 2:11-12 when he eliminated the possibility of teaching for all women.

The last three verses that appear in the context of presbyters (5:23-25) seem somewhat disconnected, but are not. The recommendation that Timothy take a little wine[15] and not just water is clearly about problems with his stomach (5:23) that could be because of stress. Timothy certainly must have felt great tension for having been sent as a delegate to a community to deal with powerful persons or "big dealers," as is commonly said.

The last two verses point to the same reality: it is important to perceive, sooner or later, the evil actions of some persons (5:24) and the good works of others (5:25). For this reason Timothy should act with discernment, to be calm and without haste in all that has to do with the naming of the leaders of the community.[16]

Here we end with what could be a reconstruction of the ecclesial structure and the situation of the community before the letter. We will now concentrate on the texts that deal with the criteria that the author establishes for leadership, and from that we will try to deduce what caused the author's discourse. We will concentrate on 3:1-12, where the requirements for the supervisor and for deacons appear. In chapter 2 we already studied the requirements for the widows.

REQUIREMENTS TO BE A SUPERVISOR: WHO IS EXCLUDED?

The Text: 1 Timothy 3:1-7

The basic questions are the following: Who are the persons capable of fulfilling the requirements presented in order to be eligible as supervisors? Could women, rich or poor, be capable of fulfilling them? Could poor men aspire to the position? Were rich men the only ones eligible? Let us look at the qualities required by the author in 3:2-7:

> ² Now a supervisor
> must be above reproach (*anepilēmpton*),
> be the husband of one wife (*mias gynaikos andra*),
> temperate (*nēphalion*),
> sensible (*sōphrona*),
> respectful (*kosmion*),
> hospitable (*philoxenon*),
> an apt teacher (*didaktikon*),
>
> ³ not a drunkard (*mē paroinon*),
> not violent (*mē plēktēn*),
> but gentle (*epieikē*),
> not quarrelsome (*amachon*),
> and not a lover of money (*aphilargyron*).
>
> ⁴ He must manage his own household well (*tou idiou oikou kalōs proïstamenon*),

keeping his children submissive (*hypotagē*)
and respectful (*semnotētos*) in every way—

⁵ for if someone does not know how to manage (*prostēnai*)
   his own household,
how can he take care (*epimelēsetai*)
of God's church (*ekklēsias*)?

⁶ He must not be a recent convert (*mē neophyton*),
or he may be puffed up with conceit and fall
into condemnation of the devil.

⁷ Moreover, he must be well thought of (*martyrian kalēn*)
   by outsiders,
so that he may not fall into disgrace (*oneidismon*)
and the snare of the devil.

The required qualities do not have much to do with the functions of a supervisor. Some commentators state that the qualities demanded are similar to those of a military general (*onosandros*), who is also called a supervisor (*episkopos*). Observe how, in the series of requirements, it is above all moral behavior that is demanded of the candidates. Only two qualities of the fifteen mentioned in the list are independent of the ethical conduct of a candidate for *episkopos*: to be apt to teach and not to be a recent convert. Neither of these, however, is exclusive to this position.

The presbyters taught, as did the widows, deacons, and the wealthy women benefactors, those who were to be excluded from the teaching (2:12). Not to be a recent convert would probably be the quality that would be the most distinct of the requisites, but it does not have to do with the central function of the supervisor. The principal problem of the Ephesian community of 1 Timothy lies in the conduct of the leaders; it is not a case of confusing functions that, according to the author, need to be restructured.

Nevertheless, if we read between the lines, the required qualities can reveal the power struggles and the proposal for their solution. To analyze each quality is not relevant, because, with the exception of some, almost all of them are clear. What is interesting to see is whether by these qualities doors are closed to some persons who have a good moral character, are prepared to teach, and are not recent converts.

The qualities of being "above reproach," "sensible," "respectable" (or "likable," *kosmion*), "temperate," "serious," "not a drunkard,"[17] "not violent," "gentle," and "peaceful" are general qualities that all members, men and women, poor and rich, should have in the Christian community; therefore, no one is excluded. Let us look now in more detail at other qualities that do merit certain reflection.

"Not a lover of money" (*aphilargyron*). This was an important quality for a supervisor, because one of the functions was to administer the money coming from donations, offerings, and so on. We know that one of the functions of the *episkopos* was to administer finances. However, deacons were also to have this attribute, although in different words: "not greedy for [ill-gotten] money" (*aischrokerdeis*). This could indicate something more than the mere honesty of the leaders. It could also be an indication of repudiation of the wealthy and greedy persons present within the community, as we have seen earlier, which relates to the struggles for power between the rich and the leaders. This appears even more clearly if we note that the term "not a lover of money" (*aphilargyron*) is repeated again in 6:10, when there is a strong criticism against those who want to keep their wealth or want to become rich, and it states that the love of money (*philargyria*) is the root of all evil. In this same context the author launches a reproach against those who think that godliness is a means of gain (6:5b). Can it be that certain benefactors who love money are being excluded? Can it be that they are trying to enter the circle of presbyters (whose honoraria the author wants to double [5:17]) in order to be supervisors? We do not really know, but we are sure that there is an indication of rejection of this kind of person, who probably caused problems in the community. The author does not want such individuals to occupy positions of leadership.

"Man or husband of one woman" (*mias gynaikos andra*) is an ambiguous term that can have two meanings. One refers to faithfulness to the wife by the husband, and the other is that the man marries only one time in his life (meaning, on becoming a widower, he will not marry again). It seems to us that the more certain meaning is his fidelity to his wife, because, for the author, marriage and the formation of the household were very important, as we have shown in previous chapters.

Now then, if this quality of masculinity is taken literally as an exclusive gender (man of one woman), automatically the women of the community remain outside the possibilities of being supervisors. For the widows, however, the same requirement is solicited, but as women ("woman of only one man," *henos andros gynē* [5:9]). We do not know for certain if with this requirement women were excluded, because we could be looking at the use of an inclusive masculine term.

It is said that the recommendation to be "hospitable" (*philoxenon*) is an exhortation directed to all members of the community. In the Hebrew Bible this was a very important ethical behavior toward the alien, the stranger.[18] In the beginning of Christianity, when the apostolate demanded an itinerate life, hospitality was essential for the founding and the visiting of the Christian communities that were dispersed among the provinces of the Roman empire. Specifically, this quality implied that a hospitable person should at least have a roof in order to offer hospitality. In ancient times, as today, people lived according to their social condition, so that there were wealthy people who lived in houses (*oikos/domus*); others lived in apartments (*insulae*) or on the street. The majority of the apartment complexes, as we saw in chapter 2, were small and dark, usually placed behind or above small shops that faced the street. Some biblical scholars think that the supervisors would have had to belong to the wealthier social classes in order to be able to have a house, so as to be able to offer hospitality. However, knowing of our humble houses in Latin America today and the generous hospitality of our poor people, in spite of their poverty, nothing impedes our thinking that in ancient times something similar happened. There could have been eligible hospitable persons with modest rented homes. Hospitality was not exclusive to the male heads of households. One of the requirements for the widows to belong to the order was that they were practicing hospitality (*exenodochēsen*, in past tense). And the slaves? Undoubtedly that depended on their masters. They could not decide on their own. It is probable that neither the slaves nor the poor without a roof could aspire to being a supervisor, with the new criteria for leadership that the author intends to impose.

"An apt teacher" (*didaktikon*). It is interesting to note that the supervisor should be a good teacher, when the traditional function of the supervisor was, above all, economic administration. There can be various reasons: one of the most important is probably the problem of "the other teaching," which, according to the author, constituted a danger to the community. Besides, as we have seen, the author of 1 Timothy wanted to give much importance to the position of supervisor. Because of this, he wants to place the supervisor at the head of the community, with the deacons as auxiliaries. The other reason is obvious: the presbyters had the task of teaching and preaching (5:17), and from them the supervisor was elected.

The quality of being "an apt teacher" does not in itself exclude anyone except the inept. Any member of the community, man or woman from any social class, could have this talent. However, if we take into account that in 2:12 the author demands that women not teach, this quality would exclude women from supervision, not because of ineptness but because of the prohibition that appears in 2:12.

The requirement that most gets our attention is the following: "He must manage his own household well (*tou idiou oikou kalōs proistamenon*) and keep his children submissive (*hypotagē*) and respectful (*semnotētos*). This requirement points to the ideology of the patriarchal household, in which the master, husband, and father must be obeyed. Here only the father is mentioned; his children must obey him. It is rare that the wife does not appear in this context, especially when there is a group of women in the community whom the author has resisted. It could be that these women lived alone and were powerful; the author does not dare to demand their obedience in the family context, but only within the church (2:11-12) because there he has official authority.

The verb used for "to manage" (*proistēmi*) also has the connotation "to keep vigil over,"[19] but in this case the connotation better fits with "to govern," "to direct," which is deduced from the mention of the obedience of the sons and daughters and by the following phrase. The sense of "to keep vigil over," "to take care of," is not absent, but is also a part of the function of the *paterfamilias*. The phrase that accompanies this required quality is very significant, because explicitly, as we saw in chapter 3, the author is transferring the values of the patriarchal household to the church, that is, the *ekklēsia* or assembly, where it is supposed that all members have the same rights and obligations, unlike the patriarchal household.[20] Greek and Latin authors saw a similarity in the patriarchal structure of the household and the structure of the city, in which the king was sovereign. The author of 1 Timothy wants to do the same, by transferring the values of the patriarchal household to the church of God. Therefore he says, without any qualms: "For, if someone does not know how to manage (*prostēnai*) his own household, how can he take care (*epimelēsetai*) of God's church (*ekklēsias*)?" (3:5).[21]

This quality demanded of the supervisor will be that which changes the direction of the original democratic organization of the *ekklēsia*. It will not only affect the women and slaves but all the liberating vision of the principles of the Reign of God proclaimed by Jesus. We do not know if this community of Timothy accepted the instructions of the letter, but we can state that in later centuries the church began to live in another manner that was hierarchical and patriarchal.

Two groups of questions come to mind upon reading this text: (1) Is it only men who govern their houses well? (2) How can we interpret the term house (*oikos*)? As the building house, from the Latin *domus* "mansion," "villa," an exclusive privilege of wealthy people? Or also home of a family whose ideology of the patriarchal household was well internalized, so that poor persons who lived in a small workshop could feel included?

With respect to the first question, it is very clear that generally it refers only to men, because it is spoken in terms of the domestic codes, which inevitably come from the patriarchal household. However, when we read in 5:14 that the young widows should marry and govern, manage, direct their households (*oikodespotein*), we can see that women also directed the domestic space; it seems as if there was a kind of division of roles and women were responsible for the management of the household slaves, if the family had them. But the master-father-husband always had the last word. If it speaks of a wealthy widow, in many cases she was the "boss," because she had taken on the role of the absent man.

Nevertheless, the intention of the author in 5:14, speaking of women governing their households, cannot be situated at the same level as in 3:4-5, since in 5:14 deals with widows who should marry again. Besides that, here the intentionality of the author is clear: to eliminate the young widows from the list of the order of widows, those who were moving in public space.

In relation to the second group of questions, relative to the significance of "house" (*oikos*), we do not believe that it deals exclusively with houses of the rich. Today we know by experience that the ideology of the patriarchal household runs through all social levels. It could perfectly well speak of a family with few resources that could have had a small workshop in which the man, his wife, and his children worked and maybe one or two slaves; it could even deal with a poor family without slaves but in which the father was seen as the head of the household, with a wife and children who were submissive and obedient. According to patriarchal ideology, he was the one who should manage well the household and watch over it.[22]

With these proposals we have come to the conclusion that if 3:4-5 excludes women in general, it does not necessarily exclude men who do not have a house (*oikos/domus*) and who live in an apartment complex (*insulae*). Here *oikos* refers more to the ideology of the patriarchal household than to the house itself. If, because of this requirement, it has been interpreted that only the rich can be supervisors, there would be a contradiction within the author himself, for, as we confirmed earlier, he did not think well of the wealthy in the Ephesian community. He needed them for their donations, but did not want them to dominate the community. He does not exclude them, of course; but he was more interested in excluding the rich women than the rich men.

Finally, we would have to say that with this requirement the itinerant preacher is excluded.[23] The quality "he must manage his own household well" reflects the importance of the family; the patriarchal household was seen as a guarantee of stability.

"He must not be a recent convert" (*mē neophyton* [3:6]). The one who would aspire to the position of supervisor (*episkopos*) should not be a neophyte. Evidently, the author thought it

important to know the tradition and the community and to have
certain experience. It is curious that the author is not explicit
about this requirement, but he notes the danger that a neophyte
could "be blinded by" or "puffed up with conceit" (*typhotheis*)
by the position, something common then and now. Thanks to
the apologetic literature of the second and third centuries, we
know that within the Gnostic currents there were recently converted people who took on leadership because their communities had a structure different from the hierarchal one. This was
criticized by the apologists.[24] It seems as if the problem in
1 Timothy is something else and is related to the struggles for
power for the leadership positions. If the reason specified by the
author to exclude the neophytes is the risk of conceit or vanity,
it is because there are probably new, powerful people who aspire
to leadership to gain more prestige. These people could be
among those who "teach another doctrine," or they could even
be the women themselves. The criticism against "the others"
could mean that "they desire to be teachers of the law, without
understanding either what they are saying . . ." (1:7). The women
benefactors who are the target of the author could also be recent
converts in the tradition and situation of the community, and
because they did not have the sympathy of some leaders, the
author includes this very objective quality for a position such as
supervisor.

The last quality, "must be well thought of by outsiders,"
shows the author's preoccupation with the surrounding Greco-
Roman society. This worry appears in other parts of the letter
(2:1-2; 5:14; 6:1). It is possible that the conduct of the supervisor was the window into the community. For that reason, the
author feared that the community would be in danger if the
supervisor did not follow the values of the society in which they
lived. In this context, a "good testimony" would have to include
a list of virtues of that culture, specifically to form a family and
manage his household well, that is, to follow the values of the
patriarchal household, values reinforced by the Roman empire.
According to the author, a "good testimony" would help him
not to "fall into discredit" (*oneidismon*) in front of those outside
of the community and "the snare of the devil" in front of those
within the community. "Snare of the devil" can mean "trap of

evil." The author, then, theologizes what is a good or bad testimony according to the values of a particular culture.

The requirement "to have a good testimony" in front of those outside is quite ample; it implies having the virtues already mentioned and certain social honor and prestige. In this case, slaves would be excluded as well as women who did not wish to marry and form a family. Not to marry was disapproved.

REQUIREMENTS TO BE DEACONS: WHO IS EXCLUDED?

The Text: 1 Timothy 3:8-12

Let us now look at the text relative to the deacons; we are changing the order of v. 11, which refers to the female deacons. The qualities of the deacons (*diakonous*) are the following:

[8] serious (*semnous*),
not double-tongued (*mē dilogous*),
not indulging in much wine (*mē oinō pollō prosechontas*),
not greedy for money (*mē aischrokerdeis*);

[9] they must hold fast to the mystery of the faith with a clear conscience (*echontas to mystērion tēs pisteōs en katharą syneidēsei*).

[10] And let them first be tested;
then, if they prove themselves blameless (*anenkletoi*),
let then serve as deacons.

[12] Let deacons be married only once (*mias gynaikos andres*),
and let them manage their children and their households well (*kalōs proïstamenoi*).

[11] Women likewise (*hōsautōs*)
must be serious (*semnas*),
not slanderers (*mē diabolous*),

but temperate (*nēphalious*),
faithful in all things (*pistas en pasin*).

Before we go on to the qualities, we must deal with the presence of the female deacons. The text shows a certain ambiguity, because in the reference to women in v. 11, the word for "deacon" does not appear, only "women likewise." This has opened the way for some scholars to say that here it does not refer to female deacons but to the wives of the male deacons. But if here it refers to the wives of the deacons, it is very strange that it does not refer to the wife of the supervisor, whose position is more important. We, along with many more scholars, believe that the verse deals with women who have the position of "deacon." The use of "likewise" (*hōsautōs*) is an indication that it refers to the same position.[25] The position of deacon is expressed in the masculine gender even when it refers to women, as in the case of Phoebe in Romans 16:1, where in Spanish it is translated in feminine. In Greek it appears in the masculine gender, because it deals precisely with an important position whose title was fixed.[26] The masculine is explained by the androcentric language of patriarchal culture. Also in Spanish (Spanish defines nouns by gender) the masculine has been used for a long time to name professions or positions carried out by women, and it has only been recently that we have begun to say "*la* ministro," "*la* medico," "*la* presidente." Even today in some parts people still use both genders to refer to women.

A difficulty for the interpretation of this text is its irregular structure; the author finishes his enumeration of the deacons' qualities, and afterwards he introduces those of the women in v. 11, and in v. 12 he returns to the male deacons. That sequence can be explained in two ways: one would consist in thinking that the author forgot to mention some qualities for the male deacons and added them in v. 12; the other is to believe that it was done deliberately: the author enumerates the qualities for the male deacons, and afterward those of the women (almost parallel with those of the deacons). After that, he intentionally adds what he considers very important, more for the male deacon than for the women who have this same responsibility: "manage their children and household well." Verse 13 would be for both genders.

It is true that the requirements for the deaconesses are very brief. It could be that the struggles for power centered more in the circle of presbyters because of the possibility that the supervisor was named from the members of that college. Perhaps the brevity was an indication that the wealthy women did not aspire to the deaconate.

Let us look in some detail at the qualities belonging to the male and female deacons.

The leadership of the deacons was also very important; the requirements are almost the same as those for the supervisor. Although the requirement of "an apt teacher" does not appear, the deacon must "hold fast to the mystery of the faith" (3:9). In the context of the plurality of teachings, the author wanted the leaders to be faithful to a certain tradition. This requirement indirectly implies that the deacons should be apt to teach. On the other hand, it is surprising that the deacons should be tested before being officially named, to prove themselves blameless (3:8). It is strange that this requirement was not among those of the supervisors, given the situation of the community. Surely they too should go through a period of testing.

The qualities that appear in v. 8 correspond to the virtues expected of a leader: serious, or dignified, not to indulge in much wine (literally "not very addicted to wine," meaning not a drunk) nor a person who says one thing to some and another thing to others (literally "of double word"). Neither should that person be a friend of greedy gain nor have bad habits. Like supervisors, deacons should not be lovers of money. Although the administration of finances was the task of the supervisors, it is possible that the deacons also managed money, because one of their important functions was that of charity. For the rest, as we have mentioned earlier, the conflicts with some benefactors made it so that the author felt it necessary to repeat this requirement about money.

The qualities for the female deacons that appear in v. 11 are almost parallel to those in v. 8 for the male deacons. They should be serious, not slanderers (*mē diabolous*), which would correspond to the case of the males to not say one thing to some and another to others (*dilogous*). Both cases deal with the control of the tongue. In respect to wine in excess, the females are told to be temperate (*nēphalious*). This quality could be literally related to drink or figuratively as a mode of being—temperate, sober.[27] The most probable connotation is the latter because modesty and moderation were two of the author's main concerns about women (2:9).

The parallelism indicates that the position, for women as well as men, was of equal importance. It is possible that this was the reality. However, in vv. 9 and 10, as mentioned earlier, to the male deacons are added two important qualities: to guard the mystery of faith and to be tested before being elected. Again our suspicions are raised. Why don't these two qualities appear for women with the position of deacon? Surely they were also tested before being elected, and one of their important qualities was to know well the message of Jesus Christ, meaning "the mystery of the faith." Verse 11 finishes by saying that they should be faithful in all things (*pistas en pasin*). Is this the equivalent of guarding the mystery of faith (*tēs pisteōs*), or does it mean simply that they should be trustworthy in all things?

Male deacons should be faithful to their wives ("husband of only one woman") and govern well their children and all who lived in their household (*kai tōn idiōn oikōn* [v. 12]). The women are not told that they should be faithful to their husbands, but that is understood. Is it understood that they are to manage their children and those who lived in their households? The young widows were counseled to marry, to create a family, and to govern their household (5:14); but in this context it would be difficult to apply such recommendations to female deacons, unless they were widows and not poor. Some scholars suspect that the females were neither married women nor widows but unmarried, dedicated to this ministry and that therefore this requirement was not given.[28]

With the expression "manage well their own households" the question arises whether only houses that had slaves, according to the author, could aspire to a position in the community, including that of deacon. We have affirmed that that was not so but could refer to persons living in apartments, including renters, but with wives and children and maybe slaves working in their own businesses. The patriarchal ideology of the submission of wives and children perfectly fits this kind of person.

Those who could not comply with this requirement were slaves[29] and the very poor, who did not have a stable dwelling place. The instruction, however, does not correspond to reality, because proof has been found that there were female slave deacons.[30] This means that, before poor women and slaves could be deacons, the author, without proposing it, closes the door on them with this instruction.

As we see it, in the enumeration of the required qualities for the deacons there is no exclusion of women in general; their existence as leaders could not be hidden, even though some interpreters see them as the wives of the deacons. Nevertheless, the brevity of the requirements for women can be interpreted in two ways: that the women had the quality of seriousness and it was not even necessary to test them, or that it was an effort to place the deaconate of women on a secondary level. The second interpretation is the most likely.

In this chapter, through the analysis of the requirements for leadership in the Christian community, we have observed that, indirectly, the author was excluding women from the position of supervisor, and the poor and slaves, both men and women, from the positions of supervisor and of deacon.[31]

1 Timothy excludes women from the position of supervisor, because one of the functions is to teach. Women would be kept out because in 2:12 they are prohibited from teaching. Women and poor men, likewise male and female slaves, are also kept out of the leadership because one of the qualities is that they govern their households well. With this requirement all poor persons who do not have a house or apartment (*insula*) are indirectly excluded.

Let us remember, however, with Schüssler Fiorenza, that 1 Timothy is a prescriptive, not a descriptive letter. This means the discourse shows the desires of the author by his intent to impose requirements. The letter does not describe the organizational form of the Christian community that receives the letter. It is possible that it was different, or at least, as we have seen earlier, that the characteristics of the patriarchal household were not so marked.

An up-to-date reading of the letter should take into account this situation. We do not know what happened to this community upon receiving the letter, but we do know that at after a certain time, what was prescribed in this letter began to be part of the leadership form of the Christian communities, as is shown in the documents of the writers called the church fathers. Today it is possible to state that the way of being church and the leadership within it reflect more the prescriptions of 1 Timothy than the descriptions of the movement of Jesus, the Christ, found in the Gospels and somehow present, according to some writings, in the behavior of some young widows, who were rebellious toward the patriarchal impositions.

Conclusion

Throughout this book we have studied 1 Timothy with an attitude of openness, and at the same time we have distanced ourselves from the author. This way of approaching the text has been important, because we have been able to listen critically to what the letter says and to dialogue and debate with the text. This letter has caused much damage to women throughout its history, because it has been used blindly by those who cling to patriarchal ideology. It seems to us that indifference to or rejection of 1 Timothy does nothing more than consolidate this ideology in today's churches, because the letter continues to be used frequently.

We believe that we have achieved what we proposed. We have discovered the fascinating world in which the first Christian communities lived and have tried to understand the author's position in the midst of the patriarchal society of the Roman empire and the conflicts that resulted from the struggles for power in the Christian community of Ephesus. The rereading of the text has been too revealing for us to continue blindly affirming in a fundamentalist manner all that the text says. We have understood the complexity of the historical moment and the diverse reasons for the affirmations of the text. Upon understanding the context behind the text and the text itself, we can dissent from all those affirmations that exclude women, the poor without a roof, and slaves. We can also dissent from the hierarchical posture that is imposed and excludes, without entering into a debate with those who think otherwise. In the study we have also been able to confirm the concern of the author for that community and its mission, and we have been in accord with some points, such as that the love of money is the root of all evil, that godliness is not a means of gain—as some preachers think today—and that the leaders of the community should not be womanizers or drunks or quarrelsome or lovers of money or illicit gain.

There are many methods of analyzing a text. We have opted for an analysis of the struggles for power in the primitive Christian community—a complicated struggle owing to the mix of components such as social position, gender, and the diversity of theological postures. Our option was correct, because it permitted us better to understand the author and his discourse, to be able to dissent more solidly from the texts that depreciate and oppress women and the poor. Even more, serious study of the letter has permitted us to dissent from those institutions, traditions, and persons that use these texts to dominate and consolidate patriarchal ideology in the church, the household, and society.

We must understand, as Luise Schottroff says, that texts such as 1 Timothy form part of the Christian canon. For her and for us as well, it would be an error to eliminate them from the Bible or to conceal them. What is necessary is a new understanding of the canon; in the canon there is the Gospel and there is the history of oppressions and discriminations committed by human beings. This is because the books of the Bible are born in the midst of human history. Schottroff is right when she says, therefore, that just as the Gospel does not suffer damage when we Christians of today question the Western history of Christianity, many times stained by persecutions and discriminations, so also the Gospel does not suffer when we find these oppressive circumstantial texts in the Bible.[1]

Fortunately, in spite of the damage fundamentalist readings have caused, they have not been able to silence many women throughout so many centuries. Today there are not just a few women who dream of a different way of being church outside the patriarchal framework. Letty Russell, for example, dreams in her last book of a new ecclesiology. She describes the church as a community of Christ in which all are invited "because we are joined around the table of the hospitality of God."[2] For her, to defend the full humanity of all women "leads to the critique, reconstruction, and reinterpretation of the Christian traditions.[3] Among them is the First Letter to Timothy. From this type of letter we should learn to understand and to dissent, to formulate a new manner of being the household of God, so that all its members, men and women, can be welcomed and can be seated with joy and mutual solidarity at "the table of God's hospitality."

I finish with this precious saying of Saint Teresa of Avila:

> It seemed to me, that Saint Paul calls for the enclosure of women. That told me little, even before I heard that this was the will of God. [The Lord] said to me: "Tell them not to follow only one part of the Scriptures. Look at others and see if you will be able to venture to tie my hands." (*Cuentas de consiencia* XVI, 1571)

Appendix I

Socioeconomic Structure
of the Roman Empire*

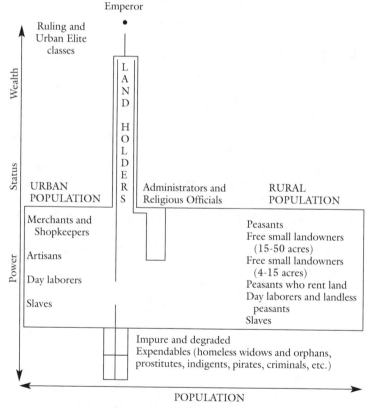

* A model proposed by G. E. Lenski and adapted by James Malcom Arlandson. According to Arlandson, the graphic model by Lenski (and others) is inadequate because by designing the figure as a diamond, it falls into the error of believing that the breach between the rich and poor was gradual. In reality, according to Arlandson, the difference between the elite and the non-elite is vast (J. M. Arlandson, *Women, Class and Society in Early Christianity* [Peabody, Mass.: Hendrickson Publishers, 1997], 22).

Appendix II

Acts of Paul and Thecla

INTRODUCTORY NOTES
BY PLUTARCO BONILLA

The Characters

When one reads this brief text, one sees that many of the names mentioned are names that also appear in the New Testament. Among those is the name of Paul, and we also find the names of Onesiphorus, Titus, Demas, Hermogenes, Alexander, and Tryphaena. Except in obvious cases, however, the characters in the apocryphal work are not necessarily to be identified with the biblical character of the same name. For example, Tryphaena in this apocryphal text is not the one found in Romans 16:12. Thecla does not appear in the biblical text; neither do the names of Simmias, Zeno, Lectra, Theocleia, Thamyris, Falconilla, or Hermias. Almost all of these names were frequently used during the first centuries, even in Rome.

Various pious women named "Thecla"[1] are mentioned in early Christian history. In this story she is known as "Thecla of Iconium." There must have existed a real Christian martyr with this name, because the worship of Saint Thecla spread in the East as well as in the West. She was the most famous of the virgin martyrs.

The "Acts"

It is probable that the events related here are a mix of real facts and pious legends. This was very common in early Christianity, when many times a fictional story was elaborated out of an original authentic nucleus. Tryphaena—Queen Tryphaena—is a historical personage (widow of the king of Thrace and mother of Polemo II, king of Pontus).[2] As is shown below, the text is preserved in diverse manuscripts, which present different endings, some of which make evident the legendary character of the narrative.

Date

Tertullian, in a work written in about the year 200, refers to the *Acts of Paul*. Hippolytus in the first half of the third century also mentions this book, as do Origen (185-254 C.E.) and Eusebius (265-339 C.E.).

The Text

The text known as *Acts of Paul and Thecla* (of which there is a Greek text) is part of a more extensive writing (*Acts of Paul*) and circulated independently of the larger work. Unfortunately, we do not have the beginning of the *Acts of Paul;* our text begins with the story of Paul leaving Antioch for Iconium.

There are various Greek manuscripts and translations of the narrative into Syriac, Coptic, and Latin. In the various versions, this small work also has different titles (such as *Acts of Paul and Thecla; Martyrdom of the Model Martyr Saint Thecla; The Passion of Saint Thecla, Virgin and Martyr*).

ACTS OF PAUL AND THECLA

From The Apocryphal New Testament, *translation and notes by M. R. James (Oxford: Clarendon, 1924). The language has been modernized.*

[1] When Paul went up to Iconium after he fled from Antioch, there journeyed with him Demas and Hermogenes the coppersmith, who were full of hypocrisy, and flattered Paul as though

they loved him. But Paul, looking only to the goodness of Christ, did them no evil, but loved them well, so that he attempted to make sweet to them all the oracles of the Lord, and of the teaching and the interpretation (of the Gospel) and of the birth and resurrection of the Beloved, and related to them word by word all the great works of Christ, as they were revealed to him.

² And a certain man named Onesiphorus, when he heard that Paul had come to Iconium, went out with his children Simmias and Zeno and his wife Lectra to meet him, so that he might receive him into his house: for Titus had told him what manner of man Paul was in appearance; for he had not seen him in the flesh, but only in the spirit.

³ And he went by the king's highway that leads to Lystra and stood expecting him, and looked upon all those who came, according to the description of Titus. And he saw Paul coming, a man little of stature, thin-haired upon the head, crooked in the legs, of good state of body, with eyebrows joining, and nose somewhat hooked, full of grace: for sometimes he appeared like a man, and sometimes he had the face of an angel.

⁴ And when Paul saw Onesiphorus he smiled, and Onesiphorus said: "Hail, you servant of the blessed God." And he said: "Grace be with you and with your house." But Demas and Hermogenes were envious, and stirred up their hypocrisy yet more, so that Demas said: "Are we not also servants of the Blessed, that you did not salute us so?" And Onesiphorus said: "I don't see in you any fruit of righteousness, but if you be such, come also into my house and refresh yourselves."

⁵ And when Paul entered into the house of Onesiphorus, there was great joy, and bowing of knees and breaking of bread, and the word of God concerning abstinence (or continence) and the resurrection; for Paul said:

> Blessed are the pure in heart, for they shall see God.
> Blessed are they that keep the flesh chaste, for they shall become the temple of God.
> Blessed are they that abstain (or the continent), for to them God shall speak.
> Blessed are they that have renounced this world, for they shall be well-pleasing to God.

Blessed are they that possess their wives as though they had them not, for they shall inherit God.

Blessed are they that have the fear of God, for they shall become angels of God.

[6] Blessed are they that tremble at the oracles of God, for they shall be comforted.

Blessed are they that receive the wisdom of Jesus Christ, for they shall be called sons of the Most High.

Blessed are they that have kept their baptism pure, for they shall rest with the Father and with the Son.

Blessed are they that have compassed the understanding of Jesus Christ, for they shall be in light.

Blessed are they that for love of God have departed from the fashion of this world, for they shall judge angels, and shall be blessed at the right hand of the Father.

Blessed are the merciful, for they shall obtain mercy and shall not see the bitter day of judgment. Blessed are the bodies of the virgins, for they shall be well-pleasing to God and shall not lose the reward of their continence (chastity), for the word of the Father shall be to them a work of salvation in the day of his Son, and they shall have rest world without end."

[7] And as Paul was saying these things in the midst of the assembly (church) in the house of Onesiphorus, a certain virgin, Thecla, whose mother was Theocleia, and who was betrothed to a husband, Thamyris, sat at the window nearby, and listened night and day to the word concerning chastity which was spoken by Paul: and she stirred not from the window, but was led onward (or pressed onward) by faith, rejoicing exceedingly: and further, when she saw many women and virgins entering in to Paul, she also desired earnestly to be accounted worthy to stand before Paul's face and to hear the word of Christ; for she had not yet seen the appearance of Paul, but only heard his speech.

[8] Now as she remained at the window, her mother sent for Thamyris, and he came with great joy as if he were already to take her to wife. Thamyris therefore said to Theocleia: "Where is my Thecla?" And Theocleia said: "I have a new tale to tell you, Thamyris: for three days and three nights Thecla arises not from

the window, neither to eat nor to drink, but looking earnestly as it were upon a joyful spectacle, she so attends to a stranger who teaches deceitful and various words, that I marvel how the great modesty of the maiden is so hardly beset.

[9] "O Thamyris, this man is upsetting the whole city of the Iconians, and your Thecla also, for all the women and the young men go in to him and are taught by him. You must, he says, fear only one God and live chastely. And my daughter, too, like a spider at the window, bound by his words, is held by a new desire and a fearful passion: for she hangs upon the things that he speaks, and the maiden is captured. But go you to her and speak to her; for she is betrothed to you."

[10] And Thamyris went to her, both loving her and fearing because of her disturbance (ecstasy), and said: "Thecla, my betrothed, why are you sitting thus? and what passion is it that holds you in amazement; turn to your Thamyris and be ashamed." And her mother also said the same: "Thecla, why do you sit thus, looking downward, and answering nothing, but as one stricken?" And they wept grievously, Thamyris because he failed of a wife, and Theocleia of a child, and the maidservants of a mistress; there was, therefore, great confusion of mourning in the house. And while all this was so, Thecla did not turn, but paid heed only to the speech of Paul.

[11] But Thamyris leaped up and went forth into the street and watched those who went in to Paul and came out. And he saw two men arguing bitterly with one another, and said to them: "You men, tell me who you are, and who is he that is inside with you, that makes the souls of young men and maidens to err, deceiving them that there may be no marriages but they should live as they are. I promise therefore to give you much money if you will tell me of him: for I am a chief man of the city."

[12] And Demas and Hermogenes said to him: "Who this man is, we know not; but he defrauds the young men of wives and the maidens of husbands, saying: You have no resurrection otherwise, except you remain continue chaste, and defile not the flesh but keep it pure."

[13] And Thamyris said to them: "Come, you men, into my house and refresh yourselves with me." And they went to a costly banquet and much wine and great wealth and a brilliant table.

And Thamyris made them drink, for he loved Thecla and desired to take her to wife. And at the dinner Thamyris said: "Tell me, men, what is his teaching, that I also may know it, for I am not a little afflicted concerning Thecla because she so loves the stranger, and I am defrauded of my marriage."

¹⁴ And Demas and Hermogenes said: "Bring him before Castelius the governor as one who persuades the multitudes with the new doctrine of the Christians; and so will he destroy him and you shall have your wife Thecla. And we will teach you of that resurrection which he asserts, that it is already come to pass in the children which we have, and we rise again when we have come to the knowledge of the true God."

¹⁵ But when Thamyris heard this of them, he was filled with envy and wrath, and rose up early and went to the house of Onesiphorus with the rulers and officers and a great crowd with staves, saying to Paul: "You have destroyed the city of the Iconians and her that was espoused to me, so that she will not have me: let us go to Castelius the governor." And all the multitude said: "Away with the wizard, for he has corrupted all our wives." And the multitude rose up together against him.

¹⁶ And Thamyris, standing before the judgment seat, cried aloud and said: "O proconsul, this is the man—we know not where he comes from—who will not allow maidens to marry: let him declare before you why he teaches such things." And Demas and Hermogenes said to Thamyris: "Say also that he is a Christian, and so will you destroy him." But the governor kept his mind steady, and called Paul, saying to him: "Who are you, and what do you teach? for it is no light accusation that these bring against you."

¹⁷ And Paul lifted up his voice and said: "If I am this day examined about what I teach, hear, O proconsul. The living God, the God of vengeance, the jealous God, the God who has need of nothing, but desires the salvation of men, has sent me, that I may sever them from corruption and uncleanness and all pleasure and death, that they may sin no more. For this God has sent his own Child, whom I preach and teach that men should have hope in him who alone has had compassion upon the world that was in error; that men may no more be under judgment but have faith and the fear of God and the knowledge of sobriety and the love

of truth. If then I teach the things that have been revealed to me of God, what wrong do I, O proconsul?" And the governor, having heard that, commanded Paul to be bound and taken away to prison until he should have leisure to hear him more carefully.

¹⁸ But Thecla at night took off her bracelets and gave them to the doorkeeper, and when the door was opened for her she went into the prison, and gave the jailer a mirror of silver and so went in to Paul and sat by his feet and heard the wonderful works of God. And Paul feared not at all, but walked in the confidence of God: and her faith also was increased as she kissed his chains.

¹⁹ Now when Thecla was sought by her own people and by Thamyris, she was looked for through the streets as one lost; and one of the fellow-servants of the doorkeeper told that she went out by night. And they examined the doorkeeper and he told them that she had gone to the stranger in the prison; and they went as he told them and found her as it were bound with him, in affection. And they went forth then and gathered the multitude to them and showed it to the governor.

²⁰ And he commanded Paul to be brought to the judgment seat; but Thecla rolled herself upon the place where Paul taught when he sat in the prison. And the governor commanded her also to be brought to the judgment seat, and she went exulting with joy. And when Paul was brought the second time the people cried out more vehemently: "He is a sorcerer, away with him!" But the governor heard Paul gladly concerning the holy works of Christ: and he took counsel, and called Thecla and said: "Why will you not marry Thamyris, according to the law of the Iconians?" But she stood looking earnestly upon Paul, and when she answered not, her mother Theocleia cried out, saying: "Burn the lawless one, burn her that is no bride in the midst of the theater, that all the women who have been taught by this man may be affrighted."

²¹ And the governor was greatly moved: and he scourged Paul and sent him out of the city, but Thecla he condemned to be burned. And straightway the governor arose and went to the theater: and all the multitude went forth to see the dreadful spectacle. But Thecla, as the lamb in the wilderness looks about for the shepherd, so sought for Paul: and she looked upon the multitude and saw the Lord sitting, resembling Paul, and said: "As

if I were not able to endure, Paul has come to look upon me." And she earnestly paid heed to him: but he departed into the heavens.

²² Now the boys and the maidens brought wood and hay to burn Thecla: and when she was brought in naked, the governor wept and marveled at the power that was in her. And they laid the wood, and the executioner bade her mount upon the pyre: and she, making the sign of the cross, went up upon the wood. And they lighted it, and though a great fire blazed forth, the fire took no hold on her; for God had compassion on her, and caused a sound under the earth, and a cloud overshadowed her above, full of rain and hail, and all the vessel of it was poured out so that many were in peril of death, and the fire was quenched, and Thecla was preserved.

²³ Now Paul was fasting with Onesiphorus and his wife and their children in an open sepulcher on the way whereby they go from Iconium to Daphne. And when many days were past, as they fasted, the boys said unto Paul: "We are hungry." And they had no means to buy bread, for Onesiphorus had left the goods of this world, and followed Paul with all his house. But Paul took off his upper garment and said: "Go, child, buy several loaves and bring them." And as the boy was buying, he saw his neighbor Thecla, and was astonished, and said: "Thecla, where are you going?" And she said: "I seek Paul, for I was preserved from the fire." And the boy said: "Come, I will bring you to him, for he has mourned for you and fasted now these six days."

²⁴ And when she came to the sepulcher to Paul, who had bowed his knees and was praying and saying, "O Father of Christ, let not the fire take hold on Thecla, but spare her, for she is yours," she standing behind him cried out: "O Father who made heaven and earth, the Father of your beloved child Jesus Christ, I bless you because you have preserved me from the fire, that I might see Paul." And Paul arose and saw her and said: "O God the knower of hearts, the Father of our Lord Jesus Christ, I bless you that you have speedily accomplished that which I asked of you, and have heard me."

²⁵ And there was much love within the sepulcher, for Paul rejoiced, and Onesiphorus, and all of them. And they had five loaves, and herbs, and water (and salt), and they rejoiced for the

holy works of Christ. And Thecla said to Paul: "I will cut my hair round about and follow you wherever you go." But he said: "The time is ill-favored and you are attractive: beware lest another temptation take you, worse than the first, and you endure it not but play the coward." And Thecla said: "Only give me the seal in Christ, and temptation shall not touch me." And Paul said: "Have patience, Thecla, and you shall receive the water."

²⁶ And Paul sent away Onesiphorus with all his house to Iconium, and so took Thecla and entered into Antioch: and as they entered in, a certain Syriarch, Alexander by name, saw Thecla and was enamored of her, and would have bribed (flattered) Paul with money and gifts. But Paul said: "I know not the woman of whom you speak, neither is she mine." But as he was of great power, he himself embraced her in the highway; and she endured it not, but sought after Paul and cried out bitterly, saying: "Force not the stranger, force not the handmaid of God. I am of the first of the Iconians, and because I would not marry Thamyris, I am cast out of the city." And she caught at Alexander and tore his cloak and took the wreath from his head and made him a laughing-stock.

²⁷ But he at the same time loving her and being ashamed of what had befallen him, brought her before the governor; and when she confessed that she had done this, he condemned her to the beasts. But the women were greatly amazed, and cried out at the judgment seat: "An evil judgment, an impious judgment!" And Thecla asked of the governor that she might remain a virgin until she should fight the beasts; and a certain rich queen, Tryphaena by name, whose daughter had died, took her into her keeping, and had her for a consolation.

²⁸ Now when the beasts were led in procession, they bound her to a fierce lioness, and the queen Tryphaena followed after her: but the lioness, when Thecla was set upon her, licked her feet, and all the people marveled. Now the writing (title) of her accusation was: "Guilty of sacrilege." And the women with their children cried out from above: "O God, an impious judgment comes to pass in this city." And after the procession Tryphaena took her again. For her daughter Falconilla, who was dead, had said to her in a dream: "Mother, you shall take in my stead

Thecla the stranger who is desolate, that she may pray for me and I be translated into the place of the righteous."

²⁹ When therefore Tryphaena received her after the procession, she also bewailed her because she was to fight the beasts on the morrow, and also, loving her closely as her own daughter Falconilla; and said: "Thecla, my second child, come, pray for my child that she may live for ever; for this have I seen in a dream." And she without delay lifted up her voice and said: "O my God, Son of the Most High who art in heaven, grant unto her according to her desire, that her daughter Falconilla may live forever." And after she had said this, Tryphaena bewailed her, considering that so great beauty was to be cast to the beasts.

³⁰ And when it was dawn, Alexander came to take her—for it was he who was running the show—saying: "The governor is set and the people trouble us: give to me the one who is to fight the beasts, that I may take her away." But Tryphaena cried aloud so that he fled away, saying: "A second mourning for my Falconilla comes about in my house, and there is no one to help, neither child, for she is dead, nor kinsman, for I am a widow. O God of Thecla my child, help Thecla."

³¹ And the governor sent soldiers to fetch Thecla: and Tryphaena did not leave her, but herself took her hand and led her up, saying: "I did bring my daughter Falconilla to the sepulcher; but you, Thecla, do I bring to fight the beasts." And Thecla wept bitterly and groaned to the Lord, saying: "Lord God in whom I believe, with whom I have taken refuge, that saved me from the fire, reward Tryphaena who has had pity on your handmaid, and has kept me pure."

³² There was therefore a tumult, and a voice of the beasts, and shouting of the people, and of the women who sat together, some saying: "Bring in the sacrilegious one!" and the women saying: "Away with the city for this unlawful deed! away with all us, proconsul! it is a bitter sight, an evil judgment!"

³³ But Thecla, being taken out of the hand of Tryphaena, was stripped and a girdle put upon her, and was cast into the stadium: and lions and bears were set against her. And a fierce lioness running to her lay down at her feet, and the press of women cried aloud. And a bear ran upon her; but the lioness ran and met him, and tore the bear to pieces. And again a lion, trained against

men, which was Alexander's, ran upon her, and the lioness wrestled with him and was slain along with him. And the women bewailed yet more, seeing that the lioness also that succored her was dead.

³⁴ Then did they put in many beasts, while she stood and stretched out her hands and prayed. And when she had ended her prayer, she turned and saw a great tank full of water, and said: "Now is it time that I should wash myself." And she cast herself in, saying: "In the name of Jesus Christ do I baptize myself on the last day." And all the women seeing it and all the people wept, saying: "Don't cast yourself into the water," so that even the governor wept that so great beauty should be devoured by seals. So, then, she cast herself into the water in the name of Jesus Christ; and the seals, seeing the light of a flash of fire, floated dead on the top of the water. And there was about her a cloud of fire, so that neither did the beasts touch her, nor was she seen to be naked.

³⁵ Now the women, when other more fearful beasts were put in, shrieked aloud, and some cast leaves, and others nard, others cassia, and some balsam, so that there was a multitude of odors; and all the beasts that were struck thereby were held as it were in sleep and touched Thecla not; so that Alexander said to the governor: "I have some bulls exceeding fearful, let us bind the criminal to them." And the governor frowning, allowed it, saying: "Do what you will." And they bound her by the feet between the bulls, and put hot irons under their bellies that they might be the more enraged and kill her. They then leaped forward; but the flame that burned about her, burned through the ropes, and she was as one not bound.

³⁶ But Tryphaena, standing by the arena, fainted at the entry, so that her handmaids said: "The queen Tryphaena is dead!" And the governor stopped the games and all the city was frightened, and Alexander falling at the governor's feet said: "Have mercy on me and on the city, and let the condemned go, lest the city perish with her; for if Caesar hears this, perhaps he will destroy us and the city, because his kinswoman the queen Tryphaena has died at the entry."

³⁷ And the governor called Thecla from among the beasts, and said to her: "Who are you? and what do you have about you that

not one of the beasts has touched you?" But she said: "I am the handmaid of the living God; and what I have about me—it is that I have believed in his Son in whom God is well pleased; for whose sake not one of the beasts has touched me. For he alone is the goal (or way) of salvation and the substance of life immortal; for unto them that are tossed about he is a refuge, unto the oppressed relief, unto the despairing shelter, and in a word, whosoever believeth not on him, shall not live, but die everlastingly."

[38] And when the governor heard this, he commanded garments to be brought and said: "Put on these garments." And she said: "He that clad me when I was naked among the beasts, the same in the day of judgment will clothe me with salvation." And she took the garments and put them on. And the governor immediately issued an act, saying: "I release to you Thecla the godly, the servant of God." And all the women cried out with a loud voice and as with one mouth gave praise to God, saying: "One is the God who has preserved Thecla": so that with their voice all the city shook.

[39] And Tryphaena, when she was told the good tidings, met her with many people and embraced Thecla and said: "Now do I believe that the dead are raised up: now do I believe that my child lives: come within, and I will make you heir of all my substance." Thecla therefore went in with her and rested in her house eight days, teaching her the word of God, so that the greater part of the maid-servants also believed, and there was great joy in the house.

[40] But Thecla yearned after Paul and sought him, sending about in all places; and it was told her that he was at Myra. And she took young men and maids, and girded herself, and sewed her mantle into a cloak after the fashion of a man, and departed for Myra, and found Paul speaking the word of God, and went to him. But when he saw her and the people that were with her he was amazed, thinking to himself: "Has some other temptation come upon her?" But she perceived it, and said to him: "I have received the washing, O Paul; for he that has worked together with you in the Gospel has worked with me also unto my baptizing."

[41] And Paul took her by the hand and brought her into the

house of Hermias, and heard all things from her; so that Paul marveled much, and they that heard were confirmed, and prayed for Tryphaena. And Thecla arose and said to Paul: "I am going to Iconium." And Paul said: "Go, and teach the word of God." Now Tryphaena had sent her much apparel and gold, so that she left it with Paul for the ministry of the poor.

[42] But she herself departed for Iconium. And she entered into the house of Onesiphorus, and fell down upon the floor where Paul had sat and taught the oracles of God, and wept, saying: "O God of me and of this house, where the light shone upon me, Jesus Christ the Son of God, my helper in prison, my helper before the governors, my helper in the fire, my helper among the beasts, thou art God, and unto thee be the glory for ever. Amen."

[43] And she found Thamyris dead, but her mother living. And she saw her mother and said to her: Theocleia my mother, can you believe that the Lord lives in the heavens? for whether you desire money, the Lord will give it to you through me: or your child, lo, I am here before you." And when she had so testified, she departed for Seleucia, and after she had enlightened many with the word of God, she slept a good sleep.

Appendix III

Plurality in Primitive Christianity

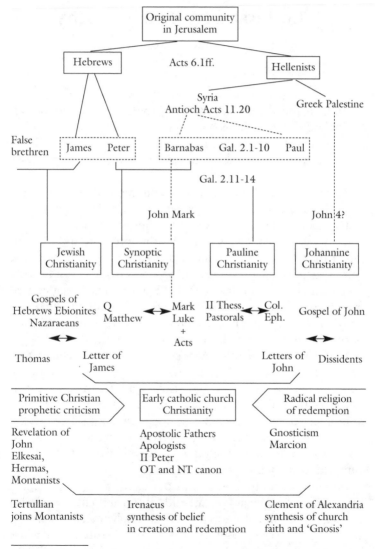

Cited from Gerd Theissen, *The Religion of the Earliest Churches* (Minneapolis: Fortress Press, 1999), 258. Used with permission.

Appendix IV

The First Letter to Timothy

(complete text)

1:1 Paul, an apostle of Christ Jesus by the command of God our Savior and of Christ Jesus our hope,

² To Timothy, my loyal child in the faith:

Grace, mercy, and peace from God the Father and Christ Jesus our Lord.

³ I urge you, as I did when I was on my way to Macedonia, to remain in Ephesus so that you may instruct certain people not to teach any different doctrine, ⁴ and not to occupy themselves with myths and endless genealogies that promote speculations rather than the divine training that is known by faith. ⁵ But the aim of such instruction is love that comes from a pure heart, a good conscience, and sincere faith. ⁶ Some people have deviated from these and turned to meaningless talk, ⁷ desiring to be teachers of the law, without understanding either what they are saying or the things about which they make assertions.

⁸ Now we know that the law is good, if one uses it legitimately. ⁹ This means understanding that the law is laid down not for the innocent but for the lawless and disobedient, for the godless and sinful, for the unholy and profane, for those who kill their father or mother, for murderers, ¹⁰ fornicators, sodomites, slave traders, liars, perjurers, and whatever else is contrary to the sound teaching ¹¹ that conforms to the glorious gospel of the blessed God, which he entrusted to me.

¹² I am grateful to Christ Jesus our Lord, who has strengthened me, because he judged me faithful and appointed me to his service, ¹³ even though I was formerly a blasphemer, a persecutor, and a man of violence. But I received mercy because I had acted ignorantly in unbelief, ¹⁴ and the grace of our Lord overflowed

for me with the faith and love that are in Christ Jesus. [15] The saying is sure and worthy of full acceptance, that Christ Jesus came into the world to save sinners—of whom I am the foremost. [16] But for that very reason I received mercy, so that in me, as the foremost, Jesus Christ might display the utmost patience, making me an example to those who would come to believe in him for eternal life. [17] To the King of the ages, immortal, invisible, the only God, be honor and glory forever and ever. Amen.

[18] I am giving you these instructions, Timothy, my child, in accordance with the prophecies made earlier about you, so that by following them you may fight the good fight, [19] having faith and a good conscience. By rejecting conscience, certain persons have suffered shipwreck in the faith; [20] among them are Hymenaeus and Alexander, whom I have turned over to Satan, so that they may learn not to blaspheme.

[2:1] First of all, then, I urge that supplications, prayers, intercessions, and thanksgivings be made for everyone, [2] for kings and all who are in high positions, so that we may lead a quiet and peaceable life in all godliness and dignity. [3] This is right and is acceptable in the sight of God our Savior, [4] who desires everyone to be saved and to come to the knowledge of the truth. [5] For there is one God; there is also one mediator between God and humankind, Christ Jesus, himself human, [6] who gave himself a ransom for all—this was attested at the right time. [7] For this I was appointed a herald and an apostle (I am telling the truth, I am not lying), a teacher of the Gentiles in faith and truth.

[8] I desire, then, that in every place the men should pray, lifting up holy hands without anger or argument; [9] also that the women should dress themselves modestly and decently in suitable clothing, not with their hair braided, or with gold, pearls, or expensive clothes, [10] but with good works, as is proper for women who profess reverence for God. [11] Let a woman learn in silence with full submission. [12] I permit no woman to teach or to have authority over a man; she is to keep silent. [13] For Adam was formed first, then Eve; [14] and Adam was not deceived, but the woman was deceived and became a transgressor. [15] Yet she will be saved through childbearing, provided they continue in faith and love and holiness, with modesty.

[3:1] The saying is sure: whoever aspires to the office of bishop desires a noble task. ² Now a bishop must be above reproach, married only once, temperate, sensible, respectable, hospitable, an apt teacher, ³ not a drunkard, not violent but gentle, not quarrelsome, and not a lover of money. ⁴ He must manage his own household well, keeping his children submissive and respectful in every way— ⁵ for if someone does not know how to manage his own household, how can he take care of God's church? ⁶ He must not be a recent convert, or he may be puffed up with conceit and fall into the condemnation of the devil. ⁷ Moreover, he must be well thought of by outsiders, so that he may not fall into disgrace and the snare of the devil.

⁸ Deacons likewise must be serious, not double-tongued, not indulging in much wine, not greedy for money; ⁹ they must hold fast to the mystery of the faith with a clear conscience. ¹⁰ And let them first be tested; then, if they prove themselves blameless, let them serve as deacons. ¹¹ Women likewise must be serious, not slanderers, but temperate, faithful in all things. ¹² Let deacons be married only once, and let them manage their children and their households well; ¹³ for those who serve well as deacons gain a good standing for themselves and great boldness in the faith that is in Christ Jesus.

¹⁴ I hope to come to you soon, but I am writing these instructions to you so that, ¹⁵ if I am delayed, you may know how one ought to behave in the household of God, which is the church of the living God, the pillar and bulwark of the truth. ¹⁶ Without any doubt, the mystery of our religion is great:

He was revealed in flesh,
    vindicated in spirit,
        seen by angels,
proclaimed among Gentiles,
    believed in throughout the world,
        taken up in glory.

⁴:¹ Now the Spirit expressly says that in later times some will renounce the faith by paying attention to deceitful spirits and teachings of demons, ² through the hypocrisy of liars whose consciences are seared with a hot iron. ³ They forbid marriage and demand abstinence from foods, which God created to be received with thanksgiving by those who believe and know the

truth. ⁴ For everything created by God is good, and nothing is to be rejected, provided it is received with thanksgiving; ⁵ for it is sanctified by God's word and by prayer.

⁶ If you put these instructions before the brothers and sisters, you will be a good servant of Christ Jesus, nourished on the words of the faith and of the sound teaching that you have followed. ⁷ Have nothing to do with profane myths and old wives' tales. Train yourself in godliness, ⁸ for, while physical training is of some value, godliness is valuable in every way, holding promise for both the present life and the life to come. ⁹ The saying is sure and worthy of full acceptance. ¹⁰ For to this end we toil and struggle, because we have our hope set on the living God, who is the Savior of all people, especially of those who believe.

¹¹ These are the things you must insist on and teach. ¹² Let no one despise your youth, but set the believers an example in speech and conduct, in love, in faith, in purity. ¹³ Until I arrive, give attention to the public reading of scripture, to exhorting, to teaching. ¹⁴ Do not neglect the gift that is in you, which was given to you through prophecy with the laying on of hands by the council of elders. ¹⁵ Put these things into practice, devote yourself to them, so that all may see your progress. ¹⁶ Pay close attention to yourself and to your teaching; continue in these things, for in doing this you will save both yourself and your hearers.

⁵:¹ Do not speak harshly to an older man, but speak to him as to a father, to younger men as brothers, ² to older women as mothers, to younger women as sisters—with absolute purity.

³ Honor widows who are really widows. ⁴ If a widow has children or grandchildren, they should first learn their religious duty to their own family and make some repayment to their parents; for this is pleasing in God's sight. ⁵ The real widow, left alone, has set her hope on God and continues in supplications and prayers night and day; ⁶ but the widow who lives for pleasure is dead even while she lives. ⁷ Give these commands as well, so that they may be above reproach. ⁸ And whoever does not provide for relatives, and especially for family members, has denied the faith and is worse than an unbeliever.

⁹ Let a widow be put on the list if she is not less than sixty years old and has been married only once; ¹⁰ she must be well attested for her good works, as one who has brought up children, shown

hospitality, washed the saints' feet, helped the afflicted, and devoted herself to doing good in every way. [11] But refuse to put younger widows on the list; for when their sensual desires alienate them from Christ, they want to marry, [12] and so they incur condemnation for having violated their first pledge. [13] Besides that, they learn to be idle, gadding about from house to house; and they are not merely idle, but also gossips and busybodies, saying what they should not say. [14] So I would have younger widows marry, bear children, and manage their households, so as to give the adversary no occasion to revile us. [15] For some have already turned away to follow Satan. [16] If any believing woman has relatives who are really widows, let her assist them; let the church not be burdened, so that it can assist those who are real widows.

[17] Let the elders who rule well be considered worthy of double honor, especially those who labor in preaching and teaching; [18] for the scripture says, "You shall not muzzle an ox while it is treading out the grain," and, "The laborer deserves to be paid." [19] Never accept any accusation against an elder except on the evidence of two or three witnesses. [20] As for those who persist in sin, rebuke them in the presence of all, so that the rest also may stand in fear. [21] In the presence of God and of Christ Jesus and of the elect angels, I warn you to keep these instructions without prejudice, doing nothing on the basis of partiality. [22] Do not ordain anyone hastily, and do not participate in the sins of others; keep yourself pure. [23] No longer drink only water, but take a little wine for the sake of your stomach and your frequent ailments. [24] The sins of some people are conspicuous and precede them to judgment, while the sins of others follow them there. [25] So also good works are conspicuous; and even when they are not, they cannot remain hidden.

[6:1] Let all who are under the yoke of slavery regard their masters as worthy of all honor, so that the name of God and the teaching may not be blasphemed. [2] Those who have believing masters must not be disrespectful to them on the ground that they are members of the church; rather they must serve them all the more, since those who benefit by their service are believers and beloved.

Teach and urge these duties. [3] Whoever teaches otherwise and does not agree with the sound words of our Lord Jesus Christ and the teaching that is in accordance with godliness, [4] is conceited, understanding nothing, and has a morbid craving for controversy and for disputes about words. From these come envy, dissension, slander, base suspicions, [5] and wrangling among those who are depraved in mind and bereft of the truth, imagining that godliness is a means of gain.

[6] Of course, there is great gain in godliness combined with contentment; [7] for we brought nothing into the world, so that we can take nothing out of it; [8] but if we have food and clothing, we will be content with these. [9] But those who want to be rich fall into temptation and are trapped by many senseless and harmful desires that plunge people into ruin and destruction. [10] For the love of money is a root of all kinds of evil, and in their eagerness to be rich some have wandered away from the faith and pierced themselves with many pains.

[11] But as for you, man of God, shun all this; pursue righteousness, godliness, faith, love, endurance, gentleness. [12] Fight the good fight of the faith; take hold of the eternal life, to which you were called and for which you made the good confession in the presence of many witnesses. [13] In the presence of God, who gives life to all things, and of Christ Jesus, who in his testimony before Pontius Pilate made the good confession, I charge you [14] to keep the commandment without spot or blame until the manifestation of our Lord Jesus Christ, [15] which he will bring about at the right time—he who is the blessed and only Sovereign, the King of kings and Lord of lords. [16] It is he alone who has immortality and dwells in unapproachable light, whom no one has ever seen or can see; to him be honor and eternal dominion. Amen.

[17] As for those who in the present age are rich, command them not to be haughty, or to set their hopes on the uncertainty of riches, but rather on God who richly provides us with everything for our enjoyment. [18] They are to do good, to be rich in good works, generous, and ready to share, [19] thus storing up for themselves the treasure of a good foundation for the future, so that they may take hold of the life that really is life.

[20] Timothy, guard what has been entrusted to you. Avoid the profane chatter and contradictions of what is falsely called knowledge; [21] by professing it some have missed the mark as regards the faith.

Grace be with you.

NOTES

INTRODUCTION

1. With the term "community reading of the Bible" we are referring to the form of reading the Bible in the base Christian communities from the perspective of the excluded. In some countries it is called "popular reading of the Bible" or "pastoral reading of the Bible." In this writing we will use these three terms interchangeably.

2. Few women have tried; among them is Irene Foulkes, who works on "difficult texts" such as 1 Tim. 2:9-15 from a pastoral perspective (not published), and Cristina Conti, who rejects these same texts as part of 1 Timothy; see "Infiel es esta palabra—1 Timothy 2:9-15," *Revista de Interpretación Bíblica Latinoamericana* 37 (2000): 41-56.

3. This is the most common hermeneutical process used in popular communities. For those not familiar with it, "to see" is the analysis of reality, "to judge" is the analysis and interpretation of the biblical text, and "to act" is the practice generated by seeing and judging; to this hermeneutical process is also added "to celebrate" the Word.

4. See Elisabeth Schüssler Fiorenza, *In Memory of Her: A Feminist Theological Reconstruction of Christian Origins* (New York: Crossroad, 1983), 310.

5. The rhetorical style was used in antiquity with the intention of persuading and convincing the hearers, polarizing positions to such a degree that they might not fit reality.

6. Schüssler Fiorenza, *In Memory of Her*, 250.

7. It is said that Gal. 3:28 was a pre-Pauline formula read at the moment of baptism.

8. 1 Timothy, 2 Timothy, and Titus form what traditionally has been called "Pastoral Letters," because they mention ecclesiastical organization.

9. We recognize that the new proposals of the letters as pseudepigraphs are very interesting and useful; nevertheless, even though we use some of them in our arguments, they will not be of primary importance.

10. The new commentary of Luke Timothy Johnson inclines toward

Pauline authorship; see *Letters to Paul's Delegates; 1 Timothy, 2 Timothy, Titus* (Valley Forge, Pa.: Trinity Press International, 1996), 26.

11. A proposal raised by Dibelius; see Martin Dibelius and Hans Conzelmann, *The Pastoral Epistles* (Philadelphia: Fortress, 1972).

12. Various commentaries or books on the Pastoral Letters reply to Dibelius, suggesting other ways of understanding the accommodation to the Greco-Roman society. See Reggie McReynolds Kidd, *Wealth and Beneficence in the Pastoral Epistles: A "Bourgeois" Form of Early Christianity,* Society of Biblical Literature Dissertation Series 122 (Atlanta: Scholars Press, 1990); Roland Schwarz, *Bürgerliches Christentum im Neuen Testament? Eine Studie zu Ethik, Amt und Recht in den Pastoralbriefen* (Klosterneuburg: Österreichisches Katholisches Bibelwerk, 1983); Philip Towner, *The Goal of Our Instruction: The Structure of Theology and Ethics in the Pastoral Epistles,* Journal for the Study of the New Testament 34 (Sheffield: Sheffield Academic Press, 1989); and others.

13. Reasons based on theological contents, terminology, style, among others.

14. Because Polycarp very possibly cites the letter in his Letter to the Philippians, we could not date it after 120 CE. Polycarp's letter can be found in Spanish and Greek in Daniel Ruiz Bueno, *Padres Apostólicos. Texto bilingüe completo,* Madrid, BAC, 1957, pp. 661-671.

15. Other biblical scholars, for example, Luke Timothy Johnson, also prefer to analyze the letters independently.

16. I am using in this book the proposals that I outlined in "1 Timoteo: que problema," in *Pasos* (Costa Rica: DEI, 2000), 1-9.

17. Along the lines of Ulrich Luz, *Matthew in History: Interpretation, Influence and Effects* (Minneapolis: Fortress, 1994).

1. THE RICH AND
THE STRUGGLES FOR POWER

1. This last interpretation is feasible if we observe the continuous, not the punctual, sense of the indicative mode and present tense: *plutein* (to keep on getting rich). See Reggie McReynolds Kidd, *Wealth and Beneficence in the Pastoral Epistles: A "Bourgeois" Form of Early Christianity,* Society of Biblical Literature Dissertation Series 122 (Atlanta: Scholars Press, 1990), 96.

2. The theses of L. W. Countryman (*The Rich Christian in the Church of the Early Empire: Contradictions and Accommodations,* Texts and Studies in Religion 7 [New York: Edwin Mellen Press, 1980], on the presence and threat of the rich in the Christian communities at the end of the first century and during the second and third centuries) and Kidd (*Wealth*) on his critique of the rich have been fundamental for our approach in this section.

3. The verb "I want" or "I desire" does not appear explicitly in relation to the dress of the women but is deduced from the parallelism of the verb "I want" with its Greek infinitive "to pray," and the infinitive "to dress."

4. The majority of the commentaries place the instructions in the context of the liturgy; others, however, also with valid arguments, affirm that the instructions were directed toward everyday life. See J. M. Holmes, *Text in a Whirlwind: A Critique of Four Exegetical Devices in 1 Timothy* (Sheffield: Sheffield Academic Press, 2000). We are inclined toward the context of the worship assembly, but observe that the repercussions transcend the context.

5. See I. Howard Marshall, *The Pastoral Epistles* (Edinburgh: T & T Clark, 1999), 418.

6. Jerome D. Quinn and William C. Wacker, *The First and Second Letters to Timothy* (Grand Rapids: Eerdmans, 1995), 218.

7. In this we agree with Marco Antonio Ramos, *I Timoteo, II Timoteo y Tito* (Miami: Caribe, 1992), 191.

8. Holmes, *Text in a Whirlwind*, 62-67.

9. See Elisabeth Schüssler Fiorenza, *In Memory of Her: A Feminist Theological Reconstruction of Christian Origins* (New York: Crossroad, 1983), 249ff.

10. See Countryman, *Rich Christian*, 149ff.

11. See this warning from biblical scholars in James Malcolm Arlandson, *Women, Class and Society in Early Christianity: Models from Luke-Acts* (Peabody, Mass.: Hendrickson, 1997), 117.

12. Ibid., 22ff.; also Ekkehard W. Stegemann and Wolfgang Stegemann, *Historia social del cristianismo primitivo: Los inicios en el judaísmo y las comunidades cristianos en el mundo mediterraneo* (Estella: Verbo Divino, 2001), 86ff.

13. The indigents were those persons who depended totally on charity, as is the case today.

14. Countryman, *Rich Christian*, 89ff.

15. I. Howard Marshall affirms that the contrast is not simply between women and men, but between women and teachers who have been legitimately chosen (*Pastoral Epistles*, 455). Countryman analyzes with more detail the tension between the rich and the official leaders (*Rich Christian*, 151ff.). We believe that the stronger conflict is between the rich women who have not been officially called and the male leaders who have been officially called.

16. See the exhaustive study done on this term by Baldwin, cited by Marshall, *Pastoral Epistles*, 456.

17. Richard A. Horsley, "Introduction" in *Paul and Empire: Religion and Power in Roman Imperial Society*, ed. Richard A. Horsley (Harrisburg, Pa.: Trinity Press International, 1997).

18. An association was a bit like a club of persons with common interests that decided to meet regularly. We will speak about the associations further on.

19. Horsley, *Paul and Empire,* 91.

20. Cited by Kidd, *Wealth,* 96.

21. This is one of the most important contributions of Kidd, *Wealth,* 111ff.

22. Ibid.

23. About associations see Wayne Meeks, *The First Urban Christians. The Social World of the Apostle Paul* (New Haven: Yale University Press, 1983), 77-80; John E. Stambaugh and David L. Balch, *The New Testament in Its Social Environment,* Library of Early Christianity 2 (Philadelphia: Westminster, 1986); Peter Garnsey and Richard Saller, "Patronal Power Relations" in *Paul and Empire,* 100-103.

24. See Garnsey and Saller, "Patronal Power Relations," 101.

25. Stambaugh and Balch, *New Testament in Its Social Environment.*

26. The term to honor (*times*) here has obvious financial connotations.

27. Martin Dibelius and Hans Conzelmann, *The Pastoral Epistles: A Commentary on the Pastoral Epistles,* trans. Philip Buttolph and Adela Yarbro, Hermeneia (Philadelphia: Fortress, 1972), 91.

28. See Kidd, *Wealth,* 93ff.

29. The term *logois* in v. 3 possibly alludes to the sayings of Jesus, because it appears explicitly with the name of Jesus and the title *Cristou.* 1 Timothy 5:18 gathers some sayings of the Gospel.

30. Stobaeus, *Eclogae* 3, cited by Dibelius and Conzelmann, *Pastoral Epistles,* 85.

31. The infinitive is in the present tense, therefore the contemplated action is continuous; it can be translated as "to maintain themselves in wealth," which would identify these persons with the rich of 6:17. See Kidd, *Wealth,* 96.

32. Kidd, *Wealth,* 96.

33. John Sheid, *Religion et piété à Rome* (Paris: Albin Michel, 2001), 36.

34. Ibid.

2. THE PATRIARCHAL HOUSEHOLD AND POWER RELATIONS BETWEEN GENDERS

1. See chapter 1 above on the patronage system.

2. Carolyn Osiek and David L. Balch, *Families in the New Testament World: Households and House Churches* (Louisville, Ky.: Westminster John Knox, 1997), 216.

3. The imperial policy on the obligation of marriage appears in the Julian laws on marriage. See Mary R. Lefkowitz and Maureen B. Fant, *Women's Life in Greece and Rome* (Baltimore: John Hopkins University Press, 1992), 104ff.

4. This term appears in most of her books.

5. James M. Arlandson, *Women, Class and Society in Early Christianity: Models from Luke-Acts* (Peabody, Mass.: Hendrickson, 1997), 503.

6. Ekkehard W. Stegemann and Wolfgang Stegemann, *Historia social del cristianismo primitivo: Los inicios en el judaísmo y las communidades cristianos en el mundo mediterraneo* (Estella: Verbo Divino, 2001), 503.

7. Two excellent studies on this theme are David L. Balch, *Let Wives Be Submissive: The Domestic Code in 1 Peter,* Society of Biblical Literature Monograph Series 26 (Atlanta: Scholars Press, 1981); and David C. Verner, *The Household of God: The Social World of the Pastoral Letters,* Society of Biblical Literature Dissertation Series 71 (Chico, Calif.: Scholars Press, 1983). Balch analyzes the domestic codes that have to do with the administration of the household. Verner also analyzes those codes that go beyond the behavior in the household and have to do with the social placement of the members and names them "social station codes."

8. Aristotle, *Politics.*

9. Verner, *Household of God,* 85.

10. See ibid., 64-70.

11. Osiek and Balch, *Families in the New Testament World,* 32. The various data here presented come from Osiek and Balch; Verner, *Household of God;* Arlandson, *Women, Class and Society;* and Stegemann and Stegemann, *Historia social del cristianismo primitivo.*

12. Verner, *Household of God,* 58.

13. For a sketch of a typical Greco-Roman city, see Richard L. Rohrbaugh, "The Pre-industrial City in Luke-Acts," in *The Social World of Luke-Acts: Models for Interpretation,* ed. Jerome H. Neyrey (Peabody, Mass.: Hendrickson, 1991), 135.

14. Osiek and Balch, *Families in the New Testament World,* 215.

15. According to Osiek and Balch, in the houses of the rich can be observed "the status and its difference" between family members and between wealthy families. With certain variations, in a typical house of a rich person immediately after the entrance was a public reception area for any matter or business (*atrium*); there was a container to collect rain water. Behind this place (*atrium*), in some houses there was a large room where the owner of the house attended to his private matters and business and received the more private visitors, and, given the ample space there, the scribes (*tablinum*) and helpers could also be there. Alongside this room was a corridor (*andron*) that led to an interior garden (*peristilo*) surrounded with columns, where the luxury and sumptuousness of the house were exhibited. There were mosaics, busts of heroes or great teach-

ers or gods or other extravagant objects, depending on whether the owner was a philosopher, a devotee, or a merchant who became sufficiently rich so as to have a house of this type. In a more interior place of the house, there were one or more dining rooms (*triclinium*), according to the number and status of the family. The Romans ate reclining on cushions, looking toward the center where there was a low table. It seems as if only men ate in this posture; the children and women sat to eat. In the *triclinium* about three cushions would fit where two to five diners reclined. Some houses had one room, called the *oecus*, which was used by everyone. Service quarters such as the kitchen or storage rooms where the slaves were were neglected, dark, and dirty; at the same time bedrooms were small and dark. Frequently the houses had a store that faced the streets.

16. See Étienne Morin, *El Puerto de Roma en el siglo II de nuestra era Ostia*, trans. Seve Calleja (Bilbao: Mensajero, 1995), 34-38.

17. See the house of Diana in Ostia.

18. See Bruce J. Malina, *The New Testament World: Insights from Cultural Anthropology*, 3rd ed. (Louisville, Ky.: Westminster John Knox, 2001); David A. deSilva, *Honor, Patronage, Kinship & Purity: Unlocking New Testament Culture* (Downers Grove, Ill.: Intervarsity, 2000), 23.

19. Osiek and Balch, *Families in the New Testament World*, 216.

20. Ibid.

21. See Verner, *Household of God*, 55ff.

22. Even in the Roman empire there was in the house a corridor called *andron* (for males), which marked a public space for males. It was understood that women would stay in the back part of the house, which was private.

23. There are inscriptions by people in modest social positions in which the family praised the deceased using the same patriarchal ideal used by the wealthy families.

24. These are the apartments (*insulae*) that had four or even seven rooms such as those discovered in Ostia. See Osiek and Balch, *Families in the New Testament World*, 18.

25. Some commentators separate v. 8 from v. 9 as independent contexts; however, the Greek term *hōsautōs* ("likewise, in the same way") unites them, also the verb "I desire" and the infinitives "to pray" and "to adorn."

26. Phillip Towner, *The Goal of Our Instruction: The Structure of Theology and Ethics in the Pastoral Epistles* (Sheffield: Sheffield Academic Press, 1989), 123.

27. J. M. Holmes, *Text in a Whirlwind: A Critique of Four Exegetical Devices in 1 Timothy 2:9-15*, Journal for the Study of the New Testament Supplement 196; Studies in New Testament Greek 7 (Sheffield: Sheffield Academic Press, 2000), 59.

28. Philip Towner recognizes that, if in fact there is a sexual conno-

tation in "discretion" and "self control," behind the instruction there could have been something more that would affect the social economic divisions; see *Goal of Our Instruction*, 208.

29. George W. Knight III, *The Pastoral Epistles: A Commentary on the Greek Text*, New International Greek Testament Commentary (Grand Rapids: Eerdmans, 1992), 133.

30. Jerome D. Quinn and William C. Wacker, *The First and Second Letters to Timothy* (Grand Rapids: Eerdmans, 1995), 216.

31. See the previous chapter on the concept of "godliness."

32. The author of 1 Timothy adapts with great liberty both the domestic codes and the codes of social placement. See Verner, *Household of God*, 106ff.

33. The phrase "the saying is sure" will be discussed in chapter 4.

34. See Athalya Brenner, ed., *A Feminist Companion to Genesis*, The Feminist Companion to the Bible 3 (Sheffield: Sheffield Academic Press, 1993); Phyllis Trible, *God and the Rhetoric of Sexuality* (Philadelphia: Fortress Press, 1978), 105ff.; Elaine Pagels, *Adam, Eve, and the Serpent* (New York: Vintage Books, 1989).

35. See Knight, *Pastoral Epistles*, 144.

36. 1 Timothy 2:15 remains ambiguous, because it does not specify whether it deals with Eve or with the woman in generic terms; v. 14 passes from Eve to become woman (*gynē*). That is why some commentators insist that it deals with the same subject "Eve" (Holmes, *Text in a Whirlwind*, 293). Others believe that the subject is changed to the woman in general (G. Knight, *Commentary on the Pastoral Epistles*, ad loc.).

37. Knight, *Pastoral Epistles*, 144ff.

38. The canon was formed after 200 C.E., and was definitely closed in the fourth century. On the plurality of Christianity, see the Appendix III.

39. See Countryman, *Rich Christian*, 108-14.

40. Holmes, *Text in a Whirlwind*, 292ff.; Holmes deals with a messianic Jewish interpretation.

41. In 5:17 the meaning "support" is clear, but in 6:1 the word refers to honor. It is interesting to note that the commandment "Honor your father and mother" would mean two things. Children must respect parents and at the same time keep watch over them when they are in need.

42. It seems that in the Roman culture widows had more help from their own family members, and/or they had more claim on the goods of their deceased husband.

43. See Arlandson, *Women, Class and Society*, 71ff.

44. Textile dyers were much despised, possibly as a result of the odor they had because of their work.

45. See the epistles of Ignatius of Antioch.

46. Bonnie Bowman Thurston, *The Widows: A Women's Ministry in the Early Church* (Minneapolis: Fortress, 1989), 44-45.

47. On ecclesiastical organization, see chapter 4 below.

48. According to Jean Daniel Kaestli and Pierre Reymond, "Première Epitre à Timothée: Traduction de travail et notes" (unpublished manuscript), "it deals with those widows who benefited from the patronage of a wealthy woman and who without a doubt lived in communities outside the family structure." It is in this group, according to these authors, that the dangers and deviations were found that the author points out in 5:6 and 12-15.

49. Personal communication in our conversations and observations about this book.

50. This does not mean, as Irene Foulkes shows, that maybe some of the young widows were not ideal discreet leaders and "would take advantage of the Christian community to justify a not so praiseworthy conduct," as could happen also with some men. If this is the case, adds Foulkes, "the problem we have with the author of 1 Timothy is that to find a solution for a possible problem with some women he discredits all the women."

51. It is believed that 5:12 is related to the vow, and if a woman expressed a desire to marry, she would be condemned for breaking the first commitment. It also has been taken into account that for some moralists of antiquity, the first marriage was sacred, and a widow should honor that for the rest of her life. We are inclined toward the interpretation that they made a commitment to Christ not to marry again.

52. See Jouette M. Bassler, "The Widow's Tale: A Fresh Look at 1 Tim. 5:3-16," *Journal of Biblical Literature* 103 (1984): 33ff.

53. 1 Timothy 5:14: "to follow Satan" probably refers to heresy or deviation from the faith.

3. THEOLOGICAL POSITIONS AND THE STRUGGLES FOR POWER

1. I. Howard Marshall, *The Pastoral Epistles* (Edinburgh: T&T Clark, 1999), 42.

2. Ibid.

3. See Appendix III.

4. See Dennis Ronald MacDonald, *The Legend and the Apostle: The Battle for Paul in Story and Canon* (Philadelphia: Westminster, 1983).

5. Lewis R. Donelson, *Pseudepigraphy and Ethical Argument in the Pastoral Epistles* (Tubingen: Mohr Siebeck, 1986), 25.

6. In the Coptic Gnostic books found at Nag Hammadi there are very unusual readings of Genesis that are different from the stories of the Creator God of the Judeo-Christian tradition. For them, the creator of the material world cannot be the transcendent God, because matter is not

good, so it has to be a minor god, a demiurge. These writings also contain stories of other minor gods.

7. Referring to them as "teachers of the law" would perhaps point to certain Jewish thinkers or Judaists who leaned toward Gnosticism. By saying "they believe themselves to be," the author alludes to a feeling of superiority.

8. See MacDonald, *Legend and the Apostle*.

9. Martin Dibelius and Hans Conzelmann, *The Pastoral Epistles: A Commentary on the Pastoral Epistles*, trans. Philip Buttolph and Adela Yarbro, Hermeneia (Philadelphia: Fortress, 1972), 92.

10. Ibid., 25.

11. Yann Redalié, *Paul après Paul: Le temps, le salut, la morale selon les épîtres à Timothée et à Tite*, Le monde de la Bible 31 (Geneva: Labor y Fides, 1994), 377.

12. Some scholars see here the Gnostic tendencies of the contrary group, supposing a dualism between matter and the world of ideas. They depreciated matter and favored ideas and knowledge; God the creator of the world would then be a demiurge of a lower status. Others see in this asceticism elements of the Judaists as seen in the Pauline letters (1 Cor. 8 and Rom. 14) because they speak of this problem.

13. Kurt Rudolph, *Gnosis: The Nature and History of Gnosticism*, trans. P. W. Coxon, K. H. Kuhn, and R. McL. Wilson (New York: HarperCollins, 1987), 214ff.

14. Jouette Bassler, "The Widows' Tale: A Fresh Look at 1 Tim 5:3-16," *Journal of Biblical Literature* 103, no. 1 (1984): 23-41.

15. Philip Towner centers his investigation on this aspect: *The Goal of Our Instruction: The Structure of Theology and Ethics in the Pastoral Epistles*, Journal for the Study of the New Testament Supplement 34 (Sheffield: Sheffield Academic Press, 1989).

16. See James C. Walters, *Ethnic Issues in Paul's Letter to the Romans: Changing Self-definitions in Earliest Roman Christianity* (Valley Forge, Pa.: Trinity Press International, 1993), 56.

17. Bassler, "Widows' Tale," 32.

18. The majority of the books and commentaries on 1 Timothy analyze the theology of the three Pastoral Letters (1 and 2 Timothy and Titus). Here we will refer only to 1 Timothy, so some ideas that are considered important to the Pastoral Letters in general will be left out if they do not appear in our letter.

19. See Redalié, *Paul après Paul;* Donelson, *Pseudepigraphy;* Towner, *Goal of Our Instruction;* and Frances M. Young, *The Theology of the Pastoral Letters* (Cambridge: Cambridge University Press, 1994), among others.

20. Redalié, *Paul après Paul*.

21. Frances Young affirms: "Given the parallels, it is not surprising

to suggest that there is a deliberate placing of the worship of Christ against the worship of Caesar as the universal gospel" (*Theology of the Pastoral Letters*, 65). See also Philip Towner, "Christology in the Letters to Timothy and Titus" (unpublished manuscript).

22. This belief that the resurrection had already happened does not appear in 1 Timothy, but does in 2 Timothy 2:18; it is very probable that this belief was shared by "the others" in 1 Timothy.

23. See Redalié, *Paul après Paul*.

24. Dennis MacDonald (*Legend and the Apostle*) begins with this text to show that the author of 1 Timothy is attacking *Acts of Paul and Thecla*, an apocryphal writing written in the middle of the second century. In this sense, the First Letter to Timothy would have been written much later than we have supposed here. However, nothing precludes supposing that there could have existed other texts similar to that of Thecla at an earlier date. Appendix II contains a translation from the Greek of the *Acts of Paul and Thecla*.

25. See John Sheid, *Religion et piété à Rome* (Paris: Albin Michel, 2000).

26. *Oikonomian theou* can also be translated "divine teaching of God." If the variant (*oikodomēn*) is read as "training," "formation," the sense fits well, because the text speaks of "other teaching." See Lorenz Oberlinner, *Die Pastoralbriefe: Kommentar zum Erster Timotheusbrief* (Freiburg/Basel/Vienna: Herder, 1994). Some versions also translate it "design" or "plan of God." We prefer the sense "administration of the household of God" guided by the context of the struggles for power and the patriarchal household. Luke Timothy Johnson opts for this same translation in his commentary; see *Letters to Paul's Delegates, 1 Timothy, 2 Timothy, Titus* (Valley Forge, Pa.: Trinity Press International, 1997), 110.

27. Elisabeth Schüssler Fiorenza calls attention to the importance of this name; see *In Memory of Her: A Feminist Theological Reconstruction of Christian Origins* (New York: Crossroad, 1983), 285ff.

28. See Luis Fernando Garciá-Viana, "Vivir en el mundo según las Cartas Pastorales," *Estudios Bíblicos* 57 (1999): 327. The Pastoral Letters look to stabilize the community; the image of the church as a patriarchal household will give the church great permanence.

29. Donelson, *Pseudepigraphy*, 103. This author comes to the same conclusion about the intentions of the author to see in the church the authority that determines the limits of the way to salvation.

30. See n. 22 above.

31. Ángel Ocampo, *Los límites de tolerancia y el sujeto universal: De paradojas y bandidos* (San José: DEI, 2002), 31-70.

32. In *Acts of Paul and Thecla*, for example, Thecla must "become masculinized" to follow Paul.

33. Luise Schottroff, *Lydia's Impatient Sisters: A Feminist Social His-*

tory of Early Christianity, trans. Barbara Rumscheidt and Martin Rumscheidt (Louisville: Westminster John Knox, 1995), 33.

4. CRITERIA FOR LEADERSHIP IN THE STRUGGLES FOR POWER

1. The Greek word *presbyteros* means "elder." It can mean a position of leadership in the Christian community or the chronological age of persons. In 1 Timothy we find both meanings: elder as in age (man in 5:1 and woman *presbyteras* in 5:2) and elders or presbyters as an official position (5:17-19).

2. According to Hans von Campenhausen, the Pastoral Letters gather different traditions, some coming out of the Jewish Christian churches, where the elders were those in front of the community, while in the others composed of Gentiles, elders were the *episkopoi*. See *Ecclesiastical Authority and Spiritual Power in the Church of the First Three Centuries* (Stanford: Stanford University Press, 1969), 107. This author, who dates the Pastoral Letters to the year 150 C.E., observes already in 1 Timothy the monarchic episcopate, meaning head of all, although without the force of the letters of Ignatius of Antioch.

3. Ibid., 55ff.

4. Elisabeth Schüssler Fiorenza, *In Memory of Her: A Feminist Theological Reconstruction of Christian Origins* (New York: Crossroad, 1983), 290.

5. Various commentators mention the possibility of this college or guild of presbyters. See Jurgen Roloff, *Der Erste Brief an Timotheus*, Evangelisch-katholischer Kommentar zum Neuen Testament 15 (Neukirchen-Vluyn: Neukirchener Verlag; Zurich: Benziger, 1988), 169ff.; Jerome D. Quinn and William C. Wacker, *The First and Second Letters to Timothy* (Grand Rapids: Eerdmans, 1995), 256.

6. Ibid.

7. We have opted to begin this section in 3:1b. The text of 3:1a ("The saying is sure") can form part the previous section to emphasize the declaration about the salvation of women through childbirth. It can also appear in this section announcing the common saying of 3:1b, and in this case it would be translated, "There is a common saying." This last version gains weight if we observe the variant *anthrōpinos* in some manuscripts. See Marco Antonio Ramos, *I Timoteo, II Timoteo y Tito* (Miami: Caribe, 1992), 202. However, we prefer to place it after 2:15 because of the radical affirmation about salvation. In fact, almost all scholars observe that the phrase appears almost always with soteriological declarations (see 1 Tim. 1:15; Titus 3:8; 2 Tim. 2:11).

8. Pliny the Younger writes in a letter to Trajan: "I have believed it necessary to find out the truth concerning two female slaves called "deaconesses" (Latin *ministrae*) (*Letters* 10.96.8).

9. On the associations, see chapter 1 above.

10. The Greek words *diplēs timēs*, "to honor" and "honor and glory," possess an economic connotation "double remuneration"; this is clear from the proverb that follows.

11. Schüssler Fiorenza, *In Memory of Her*, 287.

12. L. W. Countryman, *The Rich Christian in the Church of the Early Empire: Contradictions and Accommodations*, Texts and Studies in Religion 7 (New York: Edwin Mellen Press, 1980), 167.

13. The laying on of hands is related more to the election of leaders than to the vindication of a presbyter found guilty. The laying on of hands to pardon a penitent was used later than this letter. See I. Howard Marshall, *The Pastoral Epistles* (Edinburgh: T&T Clark, 1999), 620-22.

14. "Keep these instructions" (*tauta phylaksēs*) can refer to the process in the case of accusations as well as the impartiality in the "laying on of hands."

15. With this recommendation of the wine, it is possible that the author was trying to distance Timothy from "the others," who preached abstinence from certain foods, maybe among them, wine.

16. See George W. Knight III, *The Pastoral Epistles: A Commentary on the Greek Text*, New International Greek Testament Commentary (Grand Rapids: Eerdmans, 1992), 242.

17. Although the terms "sober" (*nēphalios*) and "drunk" (*paroinos*) are related to wine, *nēphalios* can also be read as "temperate," "serious."

18. See Exod. 22:21; 23:9; Lev. 19:10; Deut. 10:19; 24:17; Ps. 146:9.

19. According to the dictionaries this verb in the middle voice means "to put at the head," "to direct," "to govern," and in the active voice means "to keep vigil over," "to help."

20. Schüssler Fiorenza, *In Memory of Her*, 284ff.

21. Here the term "to govern," "to manage or direct," appears together with another term (*epimelēsetai*) that also has the connotation of "to keep vigil over," "to take care of." The change may simply be for reasons of style.

22. See the point about the patriarchal household as an ideal of the concept of family in chapter 2.

23. Yann Redalié, *Paul après Paul: Le temps, le salut, la morale selon les epîtres a Timothée et a Tite* (Geneva: Labor et Fides, 1994), 358.

24. Tertullian criticized "the disorderliness" of the Gnostic communities, maybe Valentinians, "without authority and church discipline," which sometimes assigned important positions to women, to neophytes;

nobody knew who was who, because they had no ecclesiastical distinction (*Prascr.*, chap. 4, cited by Kurt Rudolph, *Gnosis: The Nature and History of Gnosticism,* trans. P. W. Coxon et al. [New York: HarperCollins, 1987], 216).

25. This is the opinion of the majority of commentators on 1 Timothy.

26. See Elizabeth Castelli, "Romans," in *Searching the Scriptures,* vol. 2, *A Feminist Commentary,* ed. Elisabeth Schüssler Fiorenza (New York: Crossroad, 1994), 277ff.

27. In the case of the *episkopos* in 3:2-3 the two meanings appear.

28. Quinn and Wacker, *First and Second Letters to Timothy,* 286.

29. I. Howard Marshall observes that the Greek phrase *kai tōn idiōn oikōn* ("and those of their own household"), followed afterward by children, indicates the possession of slaves; he also notices the exclusion of slaves from the deaconate (*Pastoral Epistles,* 495). If that is so, we ask ourselves if persons who did not have slaves were excluded. We believe not, for the reasons mentioned above.

30. See Pliny the Younger, *Letters* 10.96.8.

31. See the same conclusion in Schüssler Fiorenza, *In Memory of Her,* 250, with respect not only to Timothy but to all the Christian church after the first century. For her, the root of this exclusion is in the patriarchal structures of domination and submission.

CONCLUSION

1. Luise Schottroff, *Lydia's Impatient Sisters: A Feminist Social History of Early Christianity* (Louisville: Westminster John Knox, 1995), 78.

2. Letty Russell, *Church in the Round: Feminist Interpretation of the Church* (Louisville: Westminster John Knox, 1993), 14.

3. Ibid., 13.

APPENDIX II. ACTS OF PAUL AND THECLA

1. V. Saxer, "Tecla," in *Diccionario patristico y de la antiguedad cristiana,* ed. Angelo di Bernardino (Salamanca: Sigueme, 1992).

2. *The Apocryphal New Testament,* translation and notes by M. R. James (Oxford: Clarendon, 1924). According to others, Tryphaena was the wife of Polemo I and the mother of three kings (A. F. Walls, "Trifena y Trifosa," in *Nuevo diccionario bíblico* [Buenos Aires: Certeza, 1991], 1385).

Bibliography

Aristotle. *Poetics.* Translated by Malcolm Heath. New York: Penguin Classics, 1997.

Arlandson, James Malcolm. *Women, Class and Society in Early Christianity: Models from Luke-Acts.* Peabody, Mass.: Hendrickson, 1997.

Balch, David L. *Let Wives Be Submissive: The Domestic Code in 1 Peter.* Society of Biblical Literature Monograph Series 26. Atlanta: Scholars Press, 1981.

Bassler, Jouette M. "The Widows' Tale: A Fresh Look at 1 Tim 5:3-16." *Journal of Biblical Literature* 103, no. 1 (1984): 23-41.

Brenner, Athalya, ed. *A Feminist Companion to Genesis.* The Feminist Companion to the Bible, vol. 3. Sheffield: Sheffield Academic Press, 1993.

Campenhausen, Hans von. *Ecclesiastical Authority and Spiritual Power in the Church of the First Three Centuries.* Translated by J. A. Baker. Stanford: Stanford University Press, 1969.

Castelli, Elizabeth. "Romans." In *Searching the Scriptures,* vol. 2, *A Feminist Commentary,* edited by Elisabeth Schüssler Fiorenza. New York: Crossroad Publishing, 1994.

Countryman, L. W. *The Rich Christian in the Church of the Early Empire: Contradictions and Accommodations.* Texts and Studies in Religion 7. New York: Edwin Mellen Press, 1980.

deSilva, David A. *Honor, Patronage, Kinship & Purity: Unlocking New Testament Culture.* Downers Grove, Ill.: InterVarsity, 2000.

Dibelius, Martin, and Hans Conzelmann. *The Pastoral Epistles: A Commentary on the Pastoral Epistles.* Translated by Phillip Buttolph and Adela Yarbro. Hermeneia. Philadelphia: Fortress, 1972.

Donelson, Lewis R. *Pseudepigraphy and Ethical Argument in the Pastoral Epistles.* Tübingen: Mohr Siebeck, 1986.

García-Viana, Luis Fernando. "Vivir en el mundo según las Cartas Pastorales." *Estudios Bíblicos* 57 (1999): 311-29.

Garnsey, Peter, and Richard Saller. "Patronal Power Relations." In *Paul and Empire: Religion and Power in Roman Imperial Society.* Edited by Richard A. Horsley. Harrisburg, Pa.: Trinity Press International, 1997.

Holmes, J. M. *Text in a Whirlwind: A Critique of Four Exegetical Devices in 1 Timothy 2:9-15.* Journal for the Study of the New Testament Supplement 196; Studies in New Testament Greek 7. Sheffield: Sheffield Academic Press, 2000.

Horsley, Richard, ed. *Paul and Empire: Religion and Power in Roman Imperial Society.* Harrisburg, Pa.: Trinity Press International, 1997.

Johnson, Luke Timothy. *Letters to Paul's Delegates: 1 Timothy, 2 Timothy, Titus.* Valley Forge, Pa.: Trinity Press International, 1996.

Kaestli, Jean Daniel, and Pierre Reymond. "Première Epître à Timothée: Traduction de travail et notes." Unpublished manuscript.

Kidd, Reggie McReynolds. *Wealth and Beneficence in the Pastoral Epistles: A "Bourgeois" Form of Early Christianity?* Society of Biblical Literature Dissertation Series 122. Atlanta: Scholars Press, 1990.

Knight, George W., III. *The Pastoral Epistles: A Commentary on the Greek Text.* New International Greek Testament Commentary. Grand Rapids: Eerdmans, 1992.

Lefkowitz, Mary R., and Maureen B. Fant. *Women's Life in Greece and Rome.* Baltimore: Johns Hopkins University Press, 1992.

Luz, Ulrich. *Matthew in History: Interpretation, Influence and Effects.* Minneapolis: Fortress, 1994.

MacDonald, Dennis Ronald. *The Legend and the Apostle: The Battle for Paul in Story and Canon.* Philadelphia: Westminster, 1983.

Malina, Bruce. *The New Testament World: Insights from Cultural Anthropology.* 3rd ed. Louisville: Westminster John Knox, 2001.

Marshall, I. Howard. *The Pastoral Epistles.* Edinburgh: T&T Clark, 1999.

Meeks, Wayne A. *The First Urban Christians: The Social World of the Apostle Paul.* New Haven: Yale University Press, 1983.

Morin, Étienne. *El puerto de Roman en el siglo II de nuestra era Ostia.* Translated by Seve Calleja. Bilbao: Mensajero, 1995.

Neyrey, Jerome H. *The Social World of Luke-Acts: Models for Interpretation.* Peabody, Mass.: Hendrickson, 1991.

Oberlinner, Lorenz. *Die Pastoralbriefe.* Vol. 1, *Kommentar zum Erster Timotheusbrief.* Herders theologischer Kommentar zum Neuen Testament 11/2. Freiburg: Herder, 1994.

Ocampo, Ángel. *Los límites de la tolerancia y el sujeto universal. De paradojas y bandidos.* San José: DEI, 2002.

Osiek, Carolyn, and David L. Balch. *Families in the New Testament World: Households and House Churches.* Louisville: Westminster John Knox, 1997.

Pagels, Elaine. *Adam, Eve, and the Serpent.* New York: Vintage Books, 1989.

Polycarp of Smyrna. "Letter to the Philippians." In *Early Christian Fathers.* Edited by Cyril Richardson. New York: Touchstone, 1995.

Quinn, Jerome D., and William C. Wacker. *The First and Second Letters to Timothy.* Grand Rapids: Eerdmans, 1995.

Ramos, Marco Antonio. *I Timoteo, II Timoteo y Tito.* Miami: Caribe, 1992.

Redalié, Yann. *Paul après Paul: Le temps, le salut, la morale selon les épîtres à Timothée et à Tite.* Le monde de la Bible 31. Geneva: Labor et Fides, 1994.

Rohrbaugh, Richard L. "The Pre-Industrial City in Luke-Acts." In *The Social World of Luke-Acts: Models for Interpretation,* edited by Jerome H. Neyrey. Peabody, Mass.: Hendrickson, 1991.

Roloff, Jürgen. *Die Erste Brief an Timotheus.* Evangelisch-katholisher Kommentar zum Neuen Testament 15. Neukirchen-Vluyn: Neukirchener Verlag; Zurich: Benziger, 1988.

Rudolph, Kurt. *Gnosis: The Nature and History of Gnosticism.* Translated by P. W. Coxon, K. H. Kuhn, and R. McL. Wilson. New York: HarperCollins, 1987.

Ruiz Bueno, Daniel. *Padres Apostólicos: Texto bilingüe complete.* Madrid: BAC, 1967.

Russell, Letty. *Church in the Round: Feminist Interpretation of the Church.* Louisville: Westminster John Knox, 1993.

Schottroff, Luise. *Lydia's Impatient Sisters: A Feminist Social History of Early Christianity.* Louisville: Westminster John Knox, 1995.

Schüssler Fiorenza, Elisabeth. *In Memory of Her: A Feminist Theological Reconstruction of Christian Origins.* New York: Crossroad, 1983.

———. *Rhetoric and Ethic: The Politics of Biblical Studies.* Minneapolis: Fortress, 1999.

———. *Searching the Scriptures.* Volume 2, *Feminist Commentary.* New York: Crossroad, 1994.

Schwarz, Roland. *Bürgerliches Christentum im Neuen Testament? Eine Studie zu Ethik, Amt und Recht in den Pastoralbriefen.* Klosterneuburg: Österreichisches Katholisches Bibelwerk, 1983.

Sheid, John. *Religion et piété à Rome.* Paris: Albin Michel, 2001.

Stambaugh, John E., and David L. Balch. *The New Testament in Its Social Environment.* Library of Early Christianity 2. Philadelphia: Westminster, 1986.

Stegemann, Ekkehard W., and Wolfgang Stegemann. *Historia social del cristianismo primitivo. Los inicios en el judaísmo y las comunidades cristianos en el mundo meditarraneo.* Estella: Verbo Divino, 2001.

Tamez, Elsa. "1 Timoteo: ¡qué problema!" *Pasos* 97 (2001): 1-9.

———. "Las cartas de la prisión como un género literario." Unpublished work (2001).

Theissen, Gerd. *The Religion of the Earliest Churches: Creating a Symbolic World.* Minneapolis: Fortress, 1999.

Thurston, Bonnie Bowman. *The Widows: A Women's Ministry in the Early Church*. Minneapolis: Fortress, 1989.

Towner, Philip. *The Goal of Our Instruction: The Structure of Theology and Ethics in the Pastoral Epistles*. Sheffield: Sheffield Academic Press, 1989.

Trible, Phyllis. *God and the Rhetoric of Sexuality*. Philadelphia: Fortress, 1978.

Verner, David. *The Household of God: The Social World of the Pastoral Letters*. Society of Biblical Literature Dissertation Series 71. Chico, Calif.: Scholars Press, 1983.

Walters, James C. *Ethnic Issues in Paul's Letter to the Romans: Changing Self-definitions in Earliest Roman Christianity*. Valley Forge, Pa.: Trinity Press International, 1993.

Young, Frances M. *The Theology of the Pastoral Letters*. Cambridge: Cambridge University Press, 1994.

Index of Biblical Passages

Genesis
2–3   43
3   42
3:15   44

Exodus
22:21   148n18
23:9   148n18

Leviticus
10:10   148n18

Deuteronomy
10:19   148n18
24:17   148n18

Psalms
146:9   148n18

Ecclesiastes
3:1   xix
5:12-14   21

Isaiah
1:17   51

Jeremiah
49:11   51

Zechariah
7:10   51

Matthew
6:24   18
23:14   51

Mark
2:27   88
12:40   51

Luke
10:21   83
12:13-21   13
16:13   13
20:47   51

Acts
6:1   51
14:23   90
20:17   90

Romans
5   44
14   145n12
14:1–15:17   87
14:17   88
16:1   90
16:7   51

1 Corinthians
1:18   62
1:26-27   62
8   145n12

Galatians
2:28   xix
3:28   87, 137n7

Ephesians
3:17   90

Philippians
1:1   90

1 Timothy
1:1   70, 90
1:1-2   xxiv, 70, 85
1:3   xxiii, 59
1:3-4   xviii, xxiii,
                         60, 61, 77
1:3-7   xxiv
1:4   61, 77, 78, 81
1:5   61, 82
1:7   61, 104
1:8-11   xxiv, 87
1:10   xviii, 61, 81
1:12-16   80
1:12-17   xxiv
1:14   73
1:15   66, 73, 147n7
1:16   74
1:17   71
1:18   xviii, xxiii, 16, 80
1:18-20   xxiv
1:20   xviii, 75
2:1-2   xxiv, 64, 71, 104
2:1-7   66
2:1–3:13   xxiv
2:3   70
2:3-7   xxiv
2:4   62, 72, 73
2:5   19, 62, 70, 72
2:5-6   73-74
2:8   xxiv, 2, 3, 36
2:8-12   35-40
2:8-15   26, 35
2:8–3:1a   2-11
2:9   xx, 4-5, 12,
                      37-38, 108
2:9-10   xxiii, 3, 4
2:9-12   xxiv, 2, 79
2:9-15   2, 76, 137n2
2:10   38
2:11   3, 41
2:11-12   xvii, 3, 29, 36,
                      38-39, 79,
                      95, 96, 101
2:11-15   64

2:12   4, 8, 42, 43,
                      98, 101, 109
2:13   40, 41
2:13-14   3, 43
2:13-15   xxiv, 4
2:13–3:1a   40-47
2:14   40-41, 42, 44
2:15   3, 4, 41, 43,
                   44, 45, 63, 74,
                   143n36, 147n7
3:1   1, 91, 96, 147n7
3:1-7   xviii, xxiv, 26, 35,
                   65, 91, 97-105
3:1-12   97
3:2   90
3:2-3   149n27
3:2-7   97-98
3:3   24, 63
3:3-4   79
3:4   29
3:4-5   79, 103
3:4–5:12   68
3:5   102
3:6   103
3:7   68
3:8   24, 63, 92, 107
3:8-10   xxiv
3:8-12   105-10
3:9   107
3:9-10   108
3:11   xxiv, 105-6, 107
3:12-13   xxiv, 106-7, 108
3:14-15   xxiv, 39, 77, 78
3:15   80
3:16   72, 74
3:16–4:5   xxiv
4:1   46, 59, 80, 85
4:1-2   60, 65
4:1-3   xviii, 46
4:2   16
4:3   4, 24, 63, 65
4:3-4   72
4:4-5   63
4:6-16   61

4:6–5:2	xxv
4:6–6:2	xxiv
4:7	60, 74
4:8	74
4:10	62, 70, 72, 76
4:12	xvii, xxiii
4:14	xxiii, 16, 80
4:16	75
4:17	xxiii
5:1	147n1
5:1-6	7
5:1-16	26
5:2	147n1
5:3	13, 48, 83
5:3-16	xxiii, xxv, 26, 47-56
5:4	94
5:4-8	48, 52, 53
5:5	52
5:6	52, 144n48
5:9	100
5:9-10	48, 52
5:9-15	53, 91
5:11-12	63
5:11-15	48, 52
5:12	54, 144n51
5:12-15	144n48
5:12–6:9	79
5:13	54
5:14	4, 43, 46, 55, 68, 102, 103, 104, 108, 144n53
5:15	75
5:16	13, 48, 53, 94
5:17	16, 49, 77, 99, 101, 143n41
5:17-18	94
5:17-19	147n1
5:17-22	8, 92
5:17-25	xxv, 1
5:18	140n29
5:19	16
5:19-20	95
5:21-22	16, 95
5:23	xxiv, 63

5:23-25	96
6:1	68, 104, 143n41
6:1-2	xviii, xxiii, xxv, 7, 29, 64, 79
6:1-10	xxv, 1
6:3	17-18, 19, 20, 23, 39, 59
6:3-5	xxiii, xxv, 61
6:3-10	16-25
6:4	19, 20, 61
6:5	17-19, 20, 99
6:5-8	19
6:6-8	19, 20-21
6:6-19	xxv
6:9-10	xx, xxiii, 13, 19-20 17-18, 75, 99
6:11	75
6:11-16	xxv, 16, 17, 22, 61, 71, 72, 75, 80
6:12	xviii, 16
6:13-14	70, 72
6:16	18
6:17	140n31
6:17-20	xx, xxiii, xxv, 1, 7, 11-16, 17, 21, 39, 75
6:18	18
6:20	xviii, 59, 61, 81
6:20-21	xxiii, xxv
6:31	21

2 Timothy
2:11	147n7
2:18	64, 146n22

Titus
3:8	147n7

James
1:27	51
2:1-4	9
5:1-6	21

1 Peter
3:1-7	79

Index of Names and Subjects

Acts of Paul and Thecla, 60, 66-
67, 146n24
adultery by women: sanctions
against, 27-28
archaeology: and houses, 30-32
Aristotle
and domestic codes, 29
on family, 28, 29-30
asceticism: condemned in 1 Timothy, 60, 63-65
associations, 11
activities of, 14
and Christian community, 14-
16
funerary, 15
types of, 15
Augustus
Julian law of, 27-28, 30
See also marriage

Balch, David L.
on living conditions in early
Christian community, 31
on marriage, 27
on Roman empire and associations, 14-15
on wealthy households, 31
Bassler, Jouette: on patriarchal
household, 68
benefactors
sense of superiority of, 22-23
See also patronage; women:
wealthy
Bible
authority of, xix
interpretation of, xix

chērais. See widows
childbearing: salvation of women
through, 40-47
church
and "deposit" of truth, 80
as household, 39, 78-79
as institution, 87-88
leaders (*see* leaders; leadership)
meaning of word, 79
Clement: ambiguity of, toward
wealth, 7
client
and patron, 9-11
See also patronage system
clothing
expensive: instruction against,
4-7
metaphoric sense of, 38
ostentation in: and behavior,
6; contrasted with good
works, 38
collegia. See associations
Countryman, L. W.
on idea of wealth in early
communities, 7
on opponents in 1 Timothy,
17
on rich men as leaders in early
community, 95

deacons (*diakonoi*), 89, 92
meaning of term, 90
requirements for, 105-10
as supervisors, 65
women as, 91, 106-7
diakonoi (deacons). *See* deacons

domestic codes, 29-30, 34, 39-40
  imposed on church in Roman empire, 86
  not applicable in church, 79
  widows and, 53-56
Donelson, Lewis R., 60

elders (*presbyteroi*). *See* presbyters
emperor: worship of, 70-71
Ephesus
  Christian community in, 26-27; diversity of theological positions in, 58-65; power struggles in, 57-88; theological disagreements in, 77-80
  excavations of houses in, 31-32
  as location of emperor worship, 70
episkopos (supervisor). *See* supervisor
eusebeia. *See* godliness

faith: administration to be grounded in, 77-78
family (*familia*)
  Aristotelian ideas of, 28, 29-30
  government compared to, 28
  houses of, 30-32
  ideal of, 33-35
  in Greco-Roman society, 27-28
  patriarchal, 27
  See also household
First Letter to Timothy
  authoritarianism of, 86
  authority of, 57
  authorship of, xxii-xxii
  community of, xxiiii
  date of, xxii, 138n14
  and mission, 66
  structure of, xxiv-xxv

theology of, in response to conflicts, 68-80
food: ascetic attitude to, 63-65
Foulkes, Irene: on activities of widows, 53-54
freedmen
  in patriarchal household, 27
  See also household
friendship relations, 9

gender(s)
  relations between: and patriarchal household, 26-56
  and virtues, 37-38
  See also women
Gnosticism
  and "other" teaching, 60, 61
  See also teachings
God
  as Father, 70
  as Savior, 70-72
godliness (*eusebeia*)
  as condition for salvation, 73-76
  and good works, 38
  and love of money, 19
  meaning of, 23
  not a means of gain, 16-25
  as spirituality, 38
  teachings about, 19-22
  and wealthy and struggles for power, 22-25
good works: contrasted with ostentation, 38
Greco-Roman society
  accommodation to, xxii
  family in, 27-28
  friendship relations in, 9
  "honor" in, 8
  patronage system in, 9-11
  wealth in, 6-7

Hellenistic Judaism
  and "other" teaching, 60, 61
  See also teachings

honor and shame: as cultural val-
    ues, 32-33
hope: placed in God, 13
Horsley, Richard: on Roman
    imperial government,
    10
household
    behavior in, 2, 29-30
    church as, 78-79
    codes, 29-30; and Aristotle,
    29
    patriarchal, xviii, 78-79; as
    ideal, 33-35; and power
    relations between gen-
    ders, 26-56; widows and,
    47-49, 52-56 (see also pa-
    triarchal ideology; patriar-
    chal society)
houses, 30-32, 142n22
    of the rich, 141n15

insulae, 30-34
intolerance, 84-88

James, Letter of
    and care for orphans and
    widows, 51
    on rich landowners, 21-22
Jesus Christ
    appearances of, 73-74
    as Savior, 70-72
Julian law, 27-28, 30
Juvenal, 30

Kidd, Reggie McReynolds
    on exhortation to wealthy, 12,
    16
    on opponents in 1 Timothy,
    17
king: compared to paterfamilias,
    28
Knight, George W., III
    on clothing in antiquity, 37

leaders
    conflicts with wealthy believ-
    ers, 6
    qualities of, 88, 89-110
leadership
    criteria for, 89-110
    as gift of Holy Spirit, 90-91
    instruction on, xviii
    passed by ordination, 80
    positions of, in early Christian
    communities, 89-93
    women and, 83
liturgical assembly: as context of
    instruction, 35-36

marriage
    and Acts of Paul and Thecla,
    66-67
    ascetic attitude to, 63-65, 82
    in Greco-Roman society, 27
Martial, 30
maternity. See childbearing
mission, 66
money
    love of: as root of evil, 7, 13,
    18, 21; and godliness, 19;
    as sickness, 19
    teachings about, 19-22
monotheism: suspect in Roman
    empire, 66

obedience: as condition for
    option for poor, 83
Ocampo, Ángel
    on human conflicts, 84
    on tolerance, 84-85
ordination: leadership and, 80
Origen: ambiguity of, toward
    wealth, 7
Osiek, Carolyn
    on living conditions in early
    Christian community, 31
    on marriage, 27
    on wealthy households, 31

overseer (*episkopos*). *See* supervisor

paterfamilias, xviii, 26
  authority of, in household,
    29-30
  emperor as, 70
  in Greco-Roman family, 27-
    28
  king compared to, 28
  See also household
patriarchal ideology, 40-41
patriarchal society, 26-27
  cultural background of, 27-35
  marriage and procreation in,
    27
patron(s)
  and client, 9-11
  and opponents, 17
  sense of supriority of, 23-24
  See also patronage system
patronage system, 9-11, 12
  relationship of rich to, 13-14
  and tensions in community,
    26
Paul
  biography of, 80
  and salvation, 74
Plutarch, 12
Polycarp (bishop of Smyrna), 95
poor: preferential option for, 47-
    56, 81-83
power
  relations between genders and
    patriarchal household,
    26-56
  struggles for, 16: between rich
    women and male leaders,
    8-9, 94-95; between
    supervisor and college of
    presbyters, 93-97; and
    criteria for leadership, 89-
    110; and theological posi-

tions, 57-88; and wealth
  and godliness, 22-25
presbyteroi (presbyters; elders). *See*
  presbyters
presbyters (*presbyteroi*), 89
  college of, 91-92; and strug-
    gle for power, 93-97
  meaning of term, 147n1
  women as, 91

Quinn, Jerome D.: on adorn-
  ment in antiquity, 37

Redalié, Yann
  on soteriology and parenesis,
    69
Roman Empire
  associations and, 14-15
  family in, 27-28
  patronage system and, 9-11
  social conditioning of, 65-68
  suspicion of monotheism in,
    66
  wealth in, 6
Russell, Letty: on ideal church,
    112

salvation, 69-80
  through childbearing, 4, 40-
    47
  and church leaders, 77-80
  God and Jesus as saviors, 70-
    72
  godliness as condition for, 73-
    76
  meaning of, 44
  as process, 73
  universality of, 70-71
Schottroff, Luise
  on new understanding of
    canon, 112
  on patriarchalism, 86

Schüssler Fiorenza, Elisabeth
    distinguishing description and
        prescription, xx, 109
    on patrikyriarchal society, 28
    on structure of early church,
        95
Scripture
    canon of, 59-60
    interpretation of, 2-3
shame. See honor and shame
slaves, xxiii
    in patriarchal household, 27,
        29-30
    See also household
slaveowners, xxiii
social classes: tension between, 5-
    6
sophisticated reasoning: con-
        demned in 1 Timothy,
        60-63, 82-83
Stambaugh, John E.: on Roman
        empire and associations,
        14-15
supervisor (episkopos), xviii, 89-90
    meaning of episkopos, 90
    requirements for, 97-105
    as single figure, 91-92
    and struggle for power, 93-97
symposion, 28

teachings: "other," 18, 24-25,
        58-88
Tertullian: ambiguity of, toward
        wealthy, 7
Thurston, Bonnie Bowman: on
        order of widows, 51
Timothy
    as example to believers, 80
    First Letter to (see First Letter
        to Timothy)
    identity of, xxiii-xxiv
tolerance, 84-85
Towner, Philip, 70

tradition
    defense of, xviii
    as "deposit" entrusted to
        community, 62

virtues: and gender, 37-38

Wacker, William C.: on adorn-
        ment, 37
wealth
    ambiguity toward, 7
    in antiquity, 18
    in Roman Empire, 6-7
    See also wealthy; women:
        wealthy
wealthy, xxiii
    arrogance of, 12
    and Christian community, 21-
        22, 25, 76
    critique of, xx; in Gospels, 18
    false godliness of, 24
    favors of, 11-16
    and godliness and struggles
        for power, 22-25
    houses of, 30-32, 141n15,
        142n22
    and patronage system, 13-14
    seven recommendations for,
        12-14
    women. See women: wealthy
widows (chērais), xxiii
    age of, 47, 49
    in antiquity, 50-51
    conduct of, 48-49
    donations for, 52-56
    economic situation of, 48-50
    exhorted to marry, 64-65
    list of, 48-49
    ministry of, 92
    order of, 51-52, 82; and
        donations, 52-56
women
    adultery and, 27-28

associated with sex, 42

clothing of, 2, 4-7, 36-37

economically dependent on men, 50-51

exclusion of, 25, 83

hairstyles of, 4-5

honor of, 32-33

and household codes, 29-30

instructed to learn in silence, xvii

instruction of, 2-3; on behavior in household, 2

leadership and, 83, 91

not to have authority over men, xvii, 35-40

obliged by law to marry and have children, 27-28

participation of, in public activities, 28

prohibited from teaching, 3, 8-9, 35-40, 43

role of, in Christian communities, xvii

salvation of, through childbearing, 40-47

and social strata, 6

subordination of, 4; and story of the fall, 421

wealthy, xx, xxiii: activities of, 28; as benefactors, 94; critique of, xx; 7-9; dominating community, 39, 43; as oppressors, 6; as patrons, 11, 17; and struggles for power, 2-11; as widows, 53

Also of Interest

Women & Christianity
Mary T. Malone

WINNER OF TWO CATHOLIC PRESS ASSOCIATION AWARDS

Volume I
The First Thousand Years
ISBN 1-57075-366-0

"An invaluable series on the history of women in the
Christian tradition . . . well-grounded, accessible, and able to
inform even as it raises consciousness."
—*Mary Jo Weaver*

Volume II
From 1000 to the Reformation
ISBN 1-57075-398-8

"Brings to light both the persistent courage and innovative
quality of women's lives."
—*The Other Side*

Volume III
From the Reformation to the 21st Century
ISBN 1-57075-475-6

"Commands attention from everyone interested in Christian
women's history."
–*Anne M. Clifford*

Please support your local bookstore, or call 1-800-258-5838.
For a free catalogue, please write us at
Orbis Books, Box 308
Maryknoll NY 10545-0308
or visit our website at www.orbisbooks.com

Thank you for reading *Struggles for Power in Early Christianity*.